The Global SCHOOL

Connecting Classrooms and Students Around the World

William Kist

Solution Tree | Press

a division of
Solution Tree

555 North Morton Street
Bloomington, IN 47404
800.733.6786 (toll free) / 812.336.7700
FAX: 812.336.7790
email: info@solution-tree.com
solution-tree.com

Visit **go.solution-tree.com/21stcenturyskills** to access live links to the websites in this book.

Printed in the United States of America
16 15 14 13 12   2 3 4 5

Library of Congress Cataloging-in-Publication Data

Kist, William.
   The global school : connecting classrooms and students around the world / William Kist.
       p. cm.
   Includes bibliographical references and index.
   ISBN 978-1-935543-69-5 (perfect bound) -- ISBN 978-1-935543-70-1 (library edition) 1. International education--United States. 2. Multicultural education--United States. I. Title.
   LC1090.K53 2012
   370.116--dc23
                              2012019569

Solution Tree
Jeffrey C. Jones, CEO
Edmund M. Ackerman, President

Solution Tree Press
President: Douglas M. Rife
Publisher: Robert D. Clouse
Vice President of Production: Gretchen Knapp
Managing Production Editor: Caroline Wise
Senior Production Editor: Lesley Bolton
Proofreader: Elisabeth Abrams
Text and Cover Designer: Rian Anderson

This book is dedicated to the visionary teachers described in these pages—teachers whose work continues to push schools to make global connections and, in so doing, broaden and enrich the lives of their students.

And, to my newborn children, Mariel, Liam, and Vivienne, who, I hope, will get to benefit from this visionary work and be allowed and encouraged to follow their own far-flung hopes and dreams. Just as long as they let their mom and dad accompany them once in a while!

ACKNOWLEDGMENTS

I would like to thank Robb Clouse and the supportive staff at Solution Tree for encouraging me to write this book. In particular, I'd like to thank Lesley Bolton for her skillful editing. Thanks must also go to my doctoral students, Karen Andrus Toilafield and Chad Everett Allan, for being so ready to help and contribute to this book. And, of course, I want to thank the teachers who have agreed to share their work in this book. They are the true pioneers, not only of global education, but of furthering the evolution of the way we teach and learn in schools.

Finally, I want to acknowledge my own family's contribution to my interest in global issues. On my mother's side of the family, I grew up hearing stories of my great-aunt Harriet Barrington, who was a missionary in India. I remember often hearing of the awesome distances that Aunt Harriet traveled and what an indescribably rare event it was when she would come home to visit. Our family still has her Bible, complete with its damage due to exotic insects. And on my father's side of the family, it was my grandmother, Dorothy Keller, who was the globe-trotter. My first memories of airports were from taking my grandmother to catch her flights, and I often think of the fun of the 1960s- and 1970s-era airports as we would whisk her to the gate, past the stylishly attired passengers and dashing flight crew. She first started traveling after the death of our beloved step-grandfather Karl Keller. I was too young to think about how the traveling may have helped her with her grief. I only remember being excited to get to the airport to see her and, invariably, the treasures she would bring home from faraway places such as Japan and Portugal and Austria. I think about what it must have been like for Aunt Harriet and my grandmother to make such long trips before the advent of the Internet and cell phones. How did they make flight reservations? How did they cope with the slowness of communicating back home via letters and postcards? Were they afraid to be so cut off from home? Thinking of the hardships and inconveniences they endured makes me wonder what excuse we could ever give for not taking off and seeing the world. At the very least, virtually!

Solution Tree Press would like to thank the following reviewers:

Gayle Berthiaume
Consultant and Trainer
Gayle Berthiaume Consulting LLC
Big Lake, Minnesota

David Cornelius
Director, Digital Media Outreach Programs and Professor, Online Media and
    Studio Production
Walter Cronkite School of Journalism and Mass Communication, Arizona State
    University
Phoenix, Arizona

Kevin Jarrett
K–4 Technology Facilitator
Northfield Community School
Northfield, New Jersey

Andrea McKenna
Sixth- and Seventh-Grade ESL Teacher
J.O. Kelly Middle School
Springdale, Arkansas

Laurence Peters
President
Edusolutions123
Rockville, Maryland

Adina Popa
Technology Resource Teacher, International Ambassador
Loudoun Public Schools
Ashburn, Virginia

Shekema Silveri
Chair, English Language Arts
Mount Zion High School
Jonesboro, Georgia

Visit **go.solution-tree.com/21stcenturyskills**
to access live links to the websites in this book.

TABLE OF CONTENTS

CHAPTER 3

The World Across Classrooms

CHAPTER 4

The Classroom in the World

CHAPTER 5

Getting Started

ABOUT THE AUTHOR

William Kist is an associate professor at Kent State University, where he teaches literacy methods courses for preservice teachers in the area of English education in the Adolescence to Young Adult Education Program. He also teaches graduate students in curriculum and instruction.

He has been a middle school and high school language arts teacher for the Akron Public Schools; a language arts and social studies curriculum coordinator for the Medina County Schools' Educational Service Center and the Hudson City Schools; and a consultant and trainer for school districts across the United States, both independently and as a consultant for the National Council of Teachers of English.

Kist has been active on the state and national levels as a literacy educator, founding and facilitating the Ohio Language Arts Supervisors' Network and serving as director for the Commission on Media for the National Council of Teachers of English from 2007 to 2010.

Kist has written over fifty articles and book chapters and two books, *New Literacies in Action* and *The Socially Networked Classroom*. To learn more about Kist's work, visit www.williamkist.com or follow him on Twitter at http://twitter.com/williamkist.

To book William Kist for professional development, contact pd@solution-tree.com.

PREFACE

I drive down a winding, two-lane highway deep in Amish country in Ohio. I try not to stare too obviously as a horse and buggy passes me carrying a woman dressed in 18th century garb. She's accompanied by two winsome little girls, who peer out at me with steel blue eyes. The grim-faced mother keeps her eyes straight ahead. I should do the same, as this twisting road has seen its share of accidents.

I'm traveling down this old highway to observe the Black River kindergarten iPad project, in which each student will be given his or her own iPad. The project is actually going to stretch well beyond kindergarten, as the plan is for these iPads to follow the children through at least their fourth-grade years. I was contacted by Cheryl Hlavsa, curriculum director of the Black River Local School District, to see if I would be interested in following this project from the very beginning. There is an interesting paradox to this story taking place in an area so rural that there is only spotty Internet and cell phone coverage: one of the driving forces behind this project is the desire to internationalize the school. The people of Black River want their students to be in touch with the world. Putting the students in possession of the very latest in worldwide tablet technology (an iPad) is seen by district leaders as a strong statement that they are positioning these young children as future players on the international scene, with many benefits both in terms of economic well-being and quality of life.

The enrollment of Black River Local Schools is approximately 1,500 students, 97 percent of whom are white, with 31 percent categorized as economically disadvantaged. Located on Black River School Road, in a rural corner of Medina

County, the schools are set in the midst of an Amish community. None of the Amish attend the Black River schools, however. The Amish school is a white-clapboard barn-like structure, set down in what looks like the middle of a cow pasture, seemingly a million miles away from the kindergarten iPad project.

What was the impetus of this project? When I asked Superintendent Janice Wyckoff, I was surprised that her first answer had to do with internationalism. She explained that there are few libraries in the area and that many of the families in the district live so far out of town that they cannot get an Internet connection. However, even in this geographically remote area there are several local businesses that are involved in international commerce. In talking with the leaders of these enterprises, Janice became convinced that preparing the students for an increasingly global culture should be the primary goal of the district. The Black River kindergarten project grew out of this dialogue with local stakeholders.

The iPads that are to be given out were funded by a countywide sales tax, the proceeds of which could only be used for technology. Much scrutiny went into which technology would be purchased. SMART Boards have already been installed in all elementary classrooms. Much staff development has been provided to the teachers, both within the district and elsewhere, with teachers being sent to see some of the leading staff developers in the area of new applications of technology. A "tech mentor" program has been established in which certain teachers were trained as tech leaders.

The teachers, administrators, and ultimately, the school board members saw the iPad as a key tool that would enable the students to learn, from an early age, the interface increasingly essential for communicating in an increasingly connected world. As the iPhone overtakes the Blackberry as the world's favorite smartphone, the iPad, which has an interface identical to that of the iPhone, is quickly becoming the dominant tablet, one that students will probably have to learn to use meaningfully in the coming years. I also heard other reasons for using the iPad as the vehicle for this project—it's visual; it doesn't use a keyboard; it's a tool that's hard to break; it's very portable. But the key was that the iPad could open the whole world to the little boys and girls from Black River. Janice described this as a thirteen-year project, with the goal of getting the students who will graduate in June 2024 as ready as possible for functioning and even thriving in an interlinked world.

As the kindergarten students make their way through the grades, the international component to the iPad project will be ramped up. The intentions of the project are to provide students with not only global cultural awareness but also Chinese language instruction. According to a grant application submitted to a state funding agency, some of the goals of the project include:

- Develop awareness and appreciation of cultures and people beyond the boundaries of the community and country
- Learn and utilize Chinese language and culture skills in an engaging learning environment
- Expand student horizons and enhance self-confidence by allowing them the freedom to set their own learning goals

As the students move beyond kindergarten, the plans are for them to use Rosetta Stone and Zon Education as online language learning platforms to learn Mandarin Chinese. Another website that will be used is Reach the World (www .reachtheworld.org), by which students will follow the trip of a visitor to China. Although China was chosen as a focus due to its growing dominance, culturally and economically, in the world, the culture of China was not as relevant as the process for creating a climate for global education in the small district of Black River.

It is important to the Black River teachers and administrators that the parents also become part of this project and, by extension, become digital citizens of the world themselves. Therefore, it was agreed early on that the iPads would be taken home each night and on weekends by the children. The iPads would, essentially, be theirs (although they would have to turn them back in to the district probably at the end of fourth grade). Several of the teachers involved expressed the idea that not only is this project vital to their students' futures, but also to the survival of public education.

Much preparation has gone into this project. The curriculum director and teachers visited another school in which young children were using iPads. They watched YouTube videos that showed young children using iPads. Rules were set for this experimental project. Family meetings were held in August before school started to explain the project, so that everyone was clear about the intent and the procedures of the project. Of course, the team also had to find apps (software applications) for different content areas and for different reading levels. Among the apps chosen particularly for their international education uses were:

- iBooks
- Dictionary.com
- PBS for iPad
- Animals iSpy
- Weather Channel or WeatherBug
- Montessori Approach to Geography
- ABC—Magnetic Alphabet
- Yummy Burger Maker Lite Game
- Doodle Buddy for iPad

The day has arrived for distributing the iPads to the children. The students' excitement is contagious as each steps up to receive his or her iPad from teacher Alicia Toghill.

Alicia first demonstrates how to push the slide arrow to unlock the iPad and then shows the students how to open Doodle Buddy, an app from a folder called "Free Choice." She demonstrated Doodle Buddy to the children yesterday, and a surprising number of kids remember it today, quickly choosing a color to draw with and using the erase feature. Alicia walks around and presses a link on each child's iPad that results in a "sticker" pad, allowing her to check their work and give them a happy sticker, just as she would if they were drawing on paper.

In Sarah Kipp's classroom, the rules of iPad use are being discussed. She even shows the children how to walk with their iPads. After getting through these introductory comments, Sarah plugs her iPad into the projector and demonstrates how to unlock it. She explains that the apps are in folders. I notice that she uses the word *apps* and that the kids understand what she's talking about. She tells them that today they're only going to demo a couple of apps. The first one is called Glow Draw. A child notices an advertisement for *Toy Story* at the bottom of the screen. Sarah discusses this and is able to dissuade students from clicking on the ad (at least for now).

A girl begins crying. She seems frustrated. Sarah comforts her, pointing out that it's OK to make a mistake, that she herself made a mistake as she was demonstrating the iPad to the class. This seems to calm the girl, and off the class quickly goes to the next app—ABC Fun. Sarah suggests that they each try to write their names. The app allows them to use their fingers to trace the letters on the screen.

She asks them if they'd like to try a new app. Yes, they all say—well, all but little Aden. He says, "Is it almost time for lunch? I'm hungry!"

In Kellie Rhein's classroom, the students are on the floor exploring their iPads. They are helping each other, and there is much laughter and excitement as they make discoveries. It's not long before most of the adults in the room, including me, are actively involved in helping this exploration process. I try to help one student, but he's already ahead of me in figuring out what to do. The room is filled with laughter, applause, smiles, and cries of "I did it!" I only hear one teacher speak to a student about getting back to the app he's supposed to be working with.

After about thirty minutes, each of the teachers begins the process of demonstrating how to plug in the iPads to recharge them. The distribution of the iPads is complete in about an hour, and before we know it, lunchtime arrives, and the iPads are put aside. The five- and six-year-olds go about the business of midday routines, not realizing they have taken the first steps toward becoming part of a global community.

INTRODUCTION

The purpose of this book is to help schools prepare students for an increasingly flat world. As Thomas Friedman (2005) famously describes, there have been certain trends that have flattened the world, essentially bringing us closer. These trends include the increasing prevalence of access to broadband Internet connection and the common outsourcing of even personal tasks such as tax accounting. The irony, however, is that, even as we become closer to each other, we still are far apart in terms of cultural awareness and are only at the most basic level of language awareness.

The projects described in the upcoming chapters will help teachers envision ways to help their students survive and thrive in this internationalized world. These projects have been collected from teachers from the United States, Canada, Japan, and China who are overcoming barriers and using new tools—new literacies, digital literacies, and social networking—with a goal of achieving what might be described as an intercultural critical education (Myers & Eberfors, 2010). The key word is *critical*, as the projects in this book are designed to empower kids, not to speed up their absorption into "a new robotic corporate entity" (McLuhan & Powers, 1989, p. 129).

An intercultural critical education is supported by current curriculum guides. In fact, there are overlaps between the language in these curriculum manifestos and the language used by those who call for increased attention to 21st century skills.

The United States is rapidly adopting what amounts to a national curriculum—the Common Core State Standards Initiative (www.corestandards.org). As of this writing, forty-five states have adopted these new standards, which grew out of work by the National Governors Association (NGA) and the Council of Chief State School Officers (CCSSO). One of the key features of these new standards is that they have been based, partly, on international models and are internationally benchmarked: "A particular standard was included in the document only when the best available evidence indicated that its mastery was essential for college and career readiness in a twenty-first-century, globally competitive society" (National Governors Association Center for Best Practices & Council of Chief State School Officers [NGA & CCSSO], 2010).

What does this mean for the classroom teacher who wants to help his or her students become participants in an increasingly global society? Following the Common Core standards, it means giving students practice in performing "the critical reading necessary to pick carefully through the staggering amount of information available today in print and digitally" (NGA & CCSSO, 2010). Students are expected to

> actively seek the wide, deep, and thoughtful engagement with high-quality literary and informational texts that builds knowledge, enlarges experience, and broadens worldviews. They [will] reflexively demonstrate the cogent reasoning and use of evidence that is essential to both private deliberation and responsible citizenship in a democratic republic. In short, students who meet the Standards develop the skills in reading, writing, speaking, and listening that are the foundation for any creative and purposeful expression in language. (NGA & CCSSO, 2010)

The projects described in this book are designed to develop and stretch these capabilities in students.

One of the key elements of the Common Core standards is that students "come to understand other perspectives and cultures. Students [need to] appreciate that the twenty-first-century classroom and workplace are settings in which people from often widely divergent cultures and who represent diverse experiences and perspectives must learn and work together" (NGA & CCSSO, 2010). According to the standards, students are to work to achieve this international perspective via "reading and listening," becoming "able to communicate effectively with people of varied backgrounds. . . . Through reading great classic and contemporary works of literature representative of a variety of periods, cultures, and worldviews, students can vicariously inhabit worlds and have experiences much different than their own" (NGA & CCSSO, 2010). But beyond being able to understand other perspectives and cultures, it is clear that the core standards, first of all, expect students to be able to function at a higher level of cognitive complexity than they have before. In fact, one study that correlated the core standards with existing standards from other countries found a "greater emphasis on higher order cognitive demand" in the core than in some curriculum documents from other countries (Porter, McMaken, Hwang, & Yang, 2011, p. 110).

Another influential curriculum document has come from the Partnership for 21st Century Skills (www.p21.org). The very first area of focus listed under "Core Subjects and 21st Century Themes" is global awareness as defined by the following:

> Using 21st century skills to understand and address global issues, [and] learning from and working collaboratively with individuals representing diverse cultures, religions and lifestyles in a spirit of mutual respect and open dialogue in personal, work and community contexts, [and] understanding other nations and cultures, including the use of non-English languages. (Partnership for 21st Century Skills, 2011b)

The Global School provides ideas for assignments, projects, and assessments from classrooms that are already attempting to create learning activities that will promote this kind of higher-order thinking in students. These assignments and strategies move beyond an emphasis on rote memorization and position students as global meaning makers, from the earliest days of kindergarten.

This book is intended to help those educators who want to tap into the power and excitement that new forms of communicating afford us for reaching out and co-constructing a new world. What does a truly global classroom look like? Do global applications just need to be simply tacked on at the end of a lesson to give it an international context? Or are global themes most appropriately interwoven into every facet of the curriculum and instruction? The stories of teachers who have forged an international path should be instructive to those who want to try to follow, even in a limited way.

My interest in the global school began when I was a high school English teacher. Before the advent of the Internet, I experimented with video in my classroom. From there, I started a line of inquiry that has taken me from using video to supplement teaching *The Canterbury Tales* through the onset of the Internet and into explorations of a broadened conception of reading and writing. One of the first theoretical pieces I read upon starting my journey was the New London Group's (1996) "A Pedagogy of Multiliteracies." I found it to be fascinating and inspiring but ultimately frustrating. "OK, now what?" I wondered. What is the typical teacher to do with the affordances that the new media provide? This tension between theory and practice set my research agenda for the last several years.

My research has taken me to many parts of North America and to Europe as I have attempted to profile teachers and students, focusing on the line that teachers must walk between wanting to have their students succeed in a test-driven educational culture and wanting them also to be able to freely take part in the interactive, increasingly global nature of life (Kist, 2005, 2007, 2010). I've learned how visionary teachers cope with a dizzying array of changes and struggle with a digital divide due not only to lack of access but also to students who are not digital natives. Marc Prensky (2005) suggests that children who have come of age during the Internet era are more comfortable with technology due to their growing up with it, hence their *native* status as opposed to those who grew up without computers, who are *digital immigrants*. However, my work with college-age students has made me question just how adept young people are at negotiating this new media world (Kist, 2010).

For this book, I conducted interviews that focused on the trend in many new-literacies teachers to introduce an international component into their daily classroom lives. *New literacies* refers to the many forms of representation available to us today. The *new* part of *new literacies* refers to the fact that these literacies have come about as a result of new technology and often (but not always) involve reading and writing on a screen. The teachers I interviewed for this book realize the importance of using these new forms of representation to broaden our students' horizons and point toward some guiding questions for further reflection and study. What can a truly global classroom look like on a daily basis? How can this kind of teaching be implemented and with what outcomes?

The research that has led to this book coincides with the arrival of the Common Core State Standards, which attempt to prepare students to become college and career ready in a rapidly changing world. It is more imperative than ever that students read widely and reflect deeply on global issues. Fortunately, the new media make it the easiest it has ever been to connect with the world. The possibilities for classroom discussion about world events, just from a brief glance at Twitter, for instance, are limitless, and there is simply no excuse for educators to be divorced from the world when the world is so immediately at our fingertips. This book will provide scaffolding in the form of concrete ideas for assignments and rubrics for those teachers who are ready to jump into the world with their students.

The teachers profiled and interviewed in this book were selected through snowball or peer sampling (Merriam, 1998). Using criteria that came out of my original research (Kist, 2000), I have identified teachers who embrace new literacies within daily classroom life and have a desire to teach global education.

Characteristics of New-Literacies Classrooms

- New-literacies classrooms feature daily work in multiple forms of representation.
- In such classrooms, there are explicit discussions of the merits of using certain symbol systems in certain situations with much choice.
- There are think-alouds by the teacher, who models working through problems using certain symbol systems.
- Students take part in a mix of individual and collaborative activities.
- New-literacies classrooms are places of student engagement in which students report achieving Csikszentmihalyi's (1990) *flow* state.

Source: Kist, 2000.

In addition to informative and inspiring interviews, this book provides specific examples of assignments and rubrics that teachers may implement in their classrooms immediately, with very little modification or with as much modification as desired. The ideas herein can be used in most any subject area discipline.

Any educator can find an entry point that matches his or her comfort zone and resources. We begin with an exploration of views and descriptions of global education and 21st century skills in chapter 1. In chapter 2, we look at examples of small steps every teacher can make in providing a global education. We ramp up the complexity of the instructional strategies in chapter 3 and connect classrooms across the world. Chapter 4 highlights situations in which students actually physically go to foreign countries for a global education. In chapter 5, we discuss trends in global education instruction and specific steps teachers can take to globalize their classrooms.

WHAT IS GLOBAL EDUCATION?

You say goodbye, and I say hello.

The Beatles

As Kenneth Cushner and Jennifer Mahon (2009) point out, several terms are used interchangeably to refer to "global education": *multicultural education, international education, peace education,* and *culturally relevant* or *responsive education*. There are also many terms used somewhat interchangeably to connote a broadening conception of literacy, including: *new literacies, multiliteracies, multimodalities, media literacy,* and *information and communication technology* (ICT).

In guiding the interviews conducted for this book, I have used the definition of *global education* suggested by the National Council for the Social Studies (n.d.):

> The terms global education and international education are used to describe strategies for:
>
> - gaining knowledge of world cultures;
>
> - understanding the historical, geographic, economic, political, cultural, and environmental relationships among world regions and peoples;
>
> - examining the nature of cultural differences and national or regional conflicts and problems; and
>
> - acting to influence public policy and private behavior on behalf of international understanding, tolerance and empathy.

Global education and international education are complementary approaches with different emphases. The integration of both perspectives is imperative to develop the skills, knowledge, and attitudes needed for responsible participation in a democratic society and in a global community in the 21st century.

Global education focuses on the interrelated nature of conditions, issues, trends, processes, and events while international education emphasizes specific world regions, problems, and cultures. International education encompasses studies of specific areas or regions of the world as well as the in-depth examination of a single culture or some aspect of that culture, such as its history, language, literature, religion, political organization, economic system, or current issues. It also includes cross-cultural studies that use a comparative approach in the examination of the characteristics of two or more cultures. Multi-cultural education is a closely related approach that explores the interactions among differing cultures within a political region.

Global education is not a new concept. Jean Piaget (1957) is credited with identifying Comenius, a thinker from the 1600s, who first proposed the idea of a "pansophic college based on ideas of pedagogical universalism" (Cushner & Mahon, 2009, p. 305). Charles Mann (2011) comprehensively describes the beginning of the global era as being when Christopher Columbus started the Columbian Exchange in 1492. And Mann, crediting Alfred Crosby's (1986) book *Ecological Imperialism*, emphasizes that this early globalization was most crucially ecological and biological in nature. Columbus "and his crew did not voyage alone. They were accompanied by a menagerie of insects, plants, mammals, and microorganisms" (p. 9). Mann (2011) describes a jarring transculturation that has its roots in biology: "For five centuries now the crash and chaos of constant connection has been our home condition; my garden, with its parade of exotic plants, is a small example" (p. xix).

Our global culture might have had biologic roots, but these roots have grown to encompass more than the food we eat or the plants we see. Fast-forwarding a few hundred years, popular authors (Friedman, 2005; Pink, 2005) have written about the "flattening" of our world, with Friedman indicating that there are many trends that have led to a greater international connectivity than has ever been experienced before, including the outsourcing of everything from the doing of our personal taxes to the reading of our CAT scans. While some of the world is still closed, for the most part our world is increasingly open to us to explore, if not in person, then via the Internet. The internationalized world we live in is not only impacting the creative worlds of music and fashion but also our politics and certainly our economies.

Support for a Global Education

As mentioned, new curriculum frameworks in the United States have uniformly advocated for an emphasis on preparing students to be global citizens. These models have been accompanied by college readiness reports and standards that also highlight the need for high school students to be prepared to succeed in an internationalized market. Excerpts from a sampling of these documents follow.

National Curriculum Standards for Social Studies

Of course, the National Council for the Social Studies (2010) discusses the need for the social studies classroom to have an international focus. These excerpts provide some examples of that call.

> Social studies programs should include experiences that provide for the study of global connections and interdependence.
>
> Global connections have intensified and accelerated the changes faced at the local, national, and international levels. The effects are evident in rapidly changing social, economic, and political institutions and systems. World trade has expanded and technology has removed or lowered many barriers, bringing far-flung cultures, institutions, and systems together. Connections among nations and regions of the world provide opportunities as well as uncertainties. The realities of global interdependence require deeper understanding of the increasing and diverse global connections among world societies and regions.
>
> In exploring this theme, students confront questions such as: What are the different types of global connections? What global connections have existed in the past, exist currently, and are likely in the future? How do ideas spread between societies in today's interconnected world? How does this result in change in those societies? What are the other consequences of global connections? What are the benefits from and problems associated with global interdependence? How might people in different parts of the world have different perspectives on these benefits and problems? What influence has increasing global interdependence had on patterns of international migration? How should people and societies balance global connectedness with local needs? What is needed for life to thrive on an ever changing and increasingly interdependent planet?

Analyses of the costs and benefits of increased global connections, and evaluations of the tensions between national interests and global priorities, contribute to the development of possible solutions to persistent and emerging global issues. By interpreting the patterns and relationships of increased global interdependence, and its implications for different societies, cultures and institutions, students learn to examine policy alternatives that have both national and global implications.

This theme typically appears in units or courses dealing with geography, culture, economics, history, political science, government, and technology but may also draw upon the natural and physical sciences and the humanities, including literature, the arts, and languages. Through exposure to various media and first-hand experiences, young learners become aware of how things that happen in one part of the world impact other parts of the world. Within this context, students in early grades examine and explore various types of global connections as well as basic issues and concerns. They develop responsive action plans, such as becoming e-pals with a class in another part of the world. In the middle years, learners can initiate analyses of the consequences of interactions among states, nations, and world regions as they respond to global events and changes. At the high school level, students are able to think systematically about personal, national, and global decisions, and to analyze policies and actions, and their consequences. They also develop skills in addressing and evaluating critical issues such as peace, conflict, poverty, disease, human rights, trade, and global ecology. (National Council for the Social Studies, 2010)

Partnership for 21st Century Skills

From its beginning, the Partnership for 21st Century Skills has emphasized the need for students to understand the interconnectedness of our world. The following excerpt discusses the need for students to understand the environmental aspects to this interconnectedness.

Environmental Literacy

- Demonstrate knowledge and understanding of the environment and the circumstances and conditions affecting it, particularly as relates to air, climate, land, food, energy, water and ecosystems

- Demonstrate knowledge and understanding of society's impact on the natural world (e.g., population growth, population development, resource consumption rate, etc.)

- Investigate and analyze environmental issues, and make accurate conclusions about effective solutions

- Take individual and collective action towards addressing environmental challenges (e.g., participating in global actions, designing solutions that inspire action on environmental issues) (Partnership for 21st Century Skills, 2011a)

This excerpt demonstrates the economic implications of this interconnectedness.

Life and Career Skills

Today's life and work environments require far more than thinking skills and content knowledge. The ability to navigate the complex life and work environments in the globally competitive information age requires students to pay rigorous attention to developing adequate life and career skills. (Partnership for 21st Century Skills, 2011c)

National Standards for Foreign Language Education

There has always been a strong cultural education component to foreign language education, and the following excerpts from the National Standards for Foreign Language Education highlight that emphasis.

Cultures

Gain Knowledge and Understanding of Other Cultures

- Standard 2.1: Students demonstrate an understanding of the relationship between the practices and perspectives of the culture studied

- Standard 2.2: Students demonstrate an understanding of the relationship between the products and perspectives of the culture studied

Comparisons

Develop Insight into the Nature of Language and Culture

- Standard 4.1: Students demonstrate understanding of the nature of language through comparisons of the language studied and their own

- Standard 4.2: Students demonstrate understanding of the concept of culture through comparisons of the cultures studied and their own (American Council on the Teaching of Foreign Languages, n.d.)

Horizon Report

The *Horizon Report* emphasizes the collaborative element that needs to be in place for a true global education.

The world of work is increasingly collaborative, giving rise to reflection about the way student projects are structured. This trend continues from 2010 and is being driven by the increasingly global and cooperative nature of business interactions facilitated by Internet technologies. The days of isolated desk jobs are disappearing, giving way to models in which teams work actively together to address issues too far-reaching or complex for a single worker to resolve alone. Market intelligence firm IDC notes that some one billion people fit the definition of mobile workers already, and projects that fully one-third of the global workforce—1.2 billon workers—will perform their work from multiple locations by 2013. (Johnson, Smith, Willis, Levine, & Haywood, 2011)

National Education Technology Plan 2010

The need for students to compete in a global economy is touted in this excerpt from the National Education Technology Plan (NETP) 2010.

The Department of Education's mission is to promote student achievement and preparation for global competitiveness by fostering educational excellence and equal access. (U.S. Department of Education, Office of Educational Technology, 2010, back cover)

The plan also points out that providing each child with an internationalized education can improve America's competitiveness.

Education is the key to America's economic growth and prosperity and to our ability to compete in the global economy. It is the path to good jobs and higher earning power for Americans. It is necessary for our democracy to work. It fosters the cross-border, cross-cultural collaboration required to solve the most challenging problems of our time.

Under the Obama administration, education has become an urgent priority driven by two clear goals:

- We will raise the proportion of college graduates from where it now stands (around 41 percent) so that 60 percent of our population holds a two-year or four-year degree by 2020.

- We will close the achievement gap so that all students graduate from high school ready to succeed in college and careers.

These are aggressive goals and achieving them is a sizable challenge. Add to the challenge the projections of most states and the federal government of reduced revenues for the foreseeable future, and it is clear we need cost-effective and cost-saving strategies that improve learning outcomes and graduation rates for millions of Americans.

Specifically, we must embrace innovation, prompt implementation, regular evaluation, and continuous improvement. The programs and projects that work must be brought

to scale so every school has the opportunity to take advantage of their success. (U.S.
Department of Education, Office of Educational Technology, 2010, p. ix)

This excerpt of the plan points out that we know increasingly more about the ways
people learn, and this should be put to use in service of international education.

A Model of Learning Powered by Technology

The NETP presents a model of learning powered by technology, with goals and
recommendations in five essential areas: learning, assessment, teaching, infrastruc-
ture, and productivity. The plan also identifies far-reaching "grand challenge" R&D
problems that should be funded and coordinated at a national level.

The challenging and rapidly changing demands of our global economy tell us what
people need to know and who needs to learn. Advances in learning sciences show
us how people learn. Technology makes it possible for us to act on this knowledge and understanding. (U.S. Department of Education, Office of Educational
Technology, 2010, p. x)

The need to be interdisciplinary is key to fostering international education.

What and How People Need to Learn

Whether the domain is English language arts, mathematics, sciences, social studies, history, art, or music, 21st-century competencies and such expertise as critical
thinking, complex problem solving, collaboration, and multimedia communication should be woven into all content areas. These competencies are necessary
to become expert learners, which we all must be if we are to adapt to our rapidly
changing world over the course of our lives. That involves developing deep understanding within specific content areas and making the connections among them.

How we need to learn includes using the technology that professionals in various
disciplines use. Professionals routinely use the Web and tools, such as wikis, blogs,
and digital content for the research, collaboration, and communication demanded
in their jobs. They gather data and analyze the data using inquiry and visualization
tools. They use graphical and 3D modeling tools for design. For students, using
these real-world tools creates learning opportunities that allow them to grapple
with real-world problems—opportunities that prepare them to be more productive members of a globally competitive workforce. (U.S. Department of Education,
Office of Educational Technology, 2010, p. xi)

As this excerpt demonstrates, the emphasis on global education is one of the
first goals and recommendations of the plan.

Goals and Recommendations
1.0 Learning: Engage and Empower

All learners will have engaging and empowering learning experiences both in and out of school that prepare them to be active, creative, knowledgeable, and ethical participants in our globally networked society. (U.S. Department of Education, Office of Educational Technology, 2010, p. xvi)

Western and Northern Canadian Protocol

The Western and Northern Canadian Protocol (2011) also places an emphasis on global education.

A well-educated society is the prerequisite to economic success; social cohesion and personal growth and our society is changing at a rapid pace in the 21st century. Parents, communities and researchers have identified the pressing need for learners to actively contribute to their local communities and successfully participate in a knowledge-based, globalized society and economy. There is also greater awareness of an approaching era of innovation where the ability to acquire and apply competencies are keys to future success. International research in learning informs us that if our children are to be well positioned for the future, we must take advantage of the unique potential of information and communication technologies to transform the student learning experience by enabling students to become engaged thinkers, global citizens, and active participants in collaborative and social learning environments.

Global education even has its own strand throughout the social studies curriculum in the Western and Northern Canadian Protocol, emphasizing expectations such as demonstrating global interdependence and describing key international agencies that work to protect human welfare.

Mixing Critical Literacy With Global Education

Of course, not everyone views this rush to globalize so positively. Global competition is sometimes cited as a prime reason for looking at U.S. schools from a deficit model (Wagner, 2008). The entire standardized testing movement can be traced to the publication of *A Nation at Risk* (National Commission on Excellence in Education, 1983), which famously argues that our nation is as much at risk from our poor educational system as it would be if our nation were under attack from a foreign country. Naomi Klein (2000) has written about the insidious nature of international corporate branding of children and of all humans. But, if anything, these political implications of globalization and global education suggest the very real need for a critical literacy approach to teaching students whenever global education is a focus. The teachers interviewed for this book approach this focus with an intent to help their students achieve just this kind of intercultural critical literacy. This ability to view texts critically and collaboratively is a key feature of the instruction of the teachers profiled in this book.

The acknowledged founder of critical literacy, Paulo Freire (2000), worked with adults to make sure that their literacies were not in service of a power elite but were tools to use to improve their own quality of life. The teachers profiled in this book have attempted to marry a global emphasis with such needed classic critical literacy tools, putting into practice what Jamie Myers and Fredrik Eberfors (2010) describe:

> An intercultural critical literacy with mass-distributed print and media texts is essential in our increasingly multicultural and glocalized lives in which our acts of language, literacy, and media create divisions and dislikes, instead of providing opportunities to negotiate shared meaning and value through cultural differences. (p. 149)

THE WORLD WITHIN YOUR CLASSROOM

The late environmental educator Donella Meadows (1990) is the originator of the concept of "If the world were a village of 1,000 people." This was one of the first global awareness activities that I conducted in my class. I would calculate the percentages based on a traditional class of twenty-five and ask the students to group themselves according to the various populations that Meadows describes. The students were amazed to see, for example, just how small North America is in relation to the rest of the world or how few doctors or teachers there are in relation to other professions. For example, if the world were a village of twenty-five people, it would include:

- 14 Asians
- 6 Africans
- 2 Europeans
- 2 Latin Americans
- 1 from the territories of the old USSR
- 1 North American
- < 1 Australian or New Zealander
- 8 children (only 4 are immunized against preventable infectious diseases)
- 1 over the age of 65

- 5 receive 75 percent of the income
- 5 receive only 2 percent of the income
- 2 own an automobile
- 1/8 of a student is a soldier
- 7/40 of a student is a teacher
- 1/40 of a student is a doctor

This exercise was one way to bring the world into the classroom. Like many teachers who taught during the late 1980s and early 1990s, when I wanted to provide global education for my students, I was confined to using whatever basic ideas I could find in a teacher's manual, in a professional journal, or from the teacher next door. In those days, for example, if I wanted to add some international enrichment, I could show a video or perhaps bring in a guest speaker. If I were very adventurous, I might have students bring in a variety of international food. As an English teacher, my real interest in global education involved providing a context for the international literature we were reading at the time. For many teachers, even in the 21st century, any such enrichment activities may be intended to be the spoonful of sugar to make the content go down (Kist, 2005).

Now, of course, thanks not only to decades of work that has been done in the area of global education but also to technical advances such as the Internet, there is an unlimited number of strategies, texts, and other ideas for providing a global flavor at a level of depth that was simply not available before the Internet. And, as mentioned earlier, the global benchmarking that exists within the new Common Core State Standards as well as the Partnership for 21st Century Skills makes an emphasis on global education more necessary, not just as enrichment but as a way of orienting an entire school.

But a classroom doesn't have to be exceptionally wired for there to be profound global education activities. This chapter is focused on ideas that are readily available for teachers who have very limited resources or who are ready to take small steps toward providing global education. The ideas in this chapter require just one computer with Internet access in a classroom. Even though these may seem like relatively simple ideas, they begin to unlock the potential that is available in any classroom for a richer and more meaningful global focus. This is a good place to start for the teacher who wants to get a taste of the power of internationalizing a classroom.

Internationalizing Text Selections

The first step in working toward a more global curriculum is simply expanding the text selection lists to include more international titles. Of course, many teachers do not have as much freedom as they did in the past to structure their curriculum and instruction. Still, there are some spaces left, if only in the classroom library or school library, to embrace a more international text list.

Several publications are available for helping teachers find literature with an international focus, such as:

- *Across Cultures: A Guide to Multicultural Literature for Children* (East & Thomas, 2007)
- *Bookbird (A Journal of International Children's Literature)* (International Board on Books for Young People, n.d.)
- *Promoting a Global Community Through Multicultural Children's Literature* (Steiner, 2001)
- *Reading Globally, K–8: Connecting Students to the World Through Literature* (Lehman, Freeman, & Scharer, 2010)
- *The World Through Children's Books* (Stan, 2002)

Other guides for international texts include:

- 30 Multicultural Books Every Teen Should Know (Cooperative Children's Book Center, 2006; www.education.wisc.edu/ccbc/books /detailListBooks.asp?idBookLists=253)
- 50 Books About Peace and Social Justice (Cooperative Children's Book Center, 2011; www.education.wisc.edu/ccbc/books/detailListBooks .asp?idBookLists=77)
- African American Teen Fiction (Austin Public Library, 2009; www .connectedyouth.org/books/index.cfm?booklist=afam)
- Asian and Asian American Fiction (Austin Public Library, 2010a; www .connectedyouth.org/books/index.cfm?booklist=asian)
- Batchelder Award (Association for Library Service to Children, 2012; www.ala.org/alsc/awardsgrants/bookmedia/batchelderaward)
- Global Reading: Selected Literature for Children and Teens Set in Other Countries (Cooperative Children's Book Center, 2007; www.education. wisc.edu/ccbc/books/detailListBooks.asp?idBookLists=280)
- Hispanic Teen Fiction (Austin Public Library, 2010b; www. connectedyouth.org/books/index.cfm?booklist=hispanicteen)
- Historical and/or Multicultural YA Books (Literary Link, 1998; http:// theliterarylink.com/yaauthors.html)

- International Children's Digital Library (n.d.; http://en.childrenslibrary.org)
- Middle Eastern Fiction (Austin Public Library, 2010c; www .connectedyouth.org/books/index.cfm?booklist=middle)
- Multicultural Experience: Books for Teens (Skokie Public Library, 2012; www.skokie.lib.il.us/s_teens/tn_books/tn_booklists/multcult.asp)
- Notable Books for a Global Society (Children's Literature and Reading Special Interest Group, 2011; www.clrsig.org/nbgs.php)
- Outstanding International Books List (United States Board on Books for Young People, 2012; www.usbby.org/list_oibl.html)
- Text Exemplars From the Common Core State Standards (NGA & CCSSO, 2010; www.corestandards.org/assets/Appendix_B.pdf)

Visit **go.solution-tree.com/21stcenturyskills** to access live links to the websites in this book.

I spoke with master librarian Celia Huffman, youth services manager of the Cuyahoga County Public Library in Cleveland, Ohio, to get her perspective on getting kids in touch with international texts. Celia explained that her library subscribes to several online storybook database services for younger children, such as BookFlix (http://teacher.scholastic.com/products/bookflixfreetrial) and TumbleBook Library (www.tumblebooks.com/library/asp/about_tumblebooks.asp). These databases include titles of books in other languages. She also recommended Byki (www.byki.com), which includes online software for older kids who are attempting to learn a foreign language.

Like many libraries, the Cuyahoga County Library (2012) has an online homework-help page. "We call ours Got Homework?" said Celia. "[It has] information on different countries and cultures of the world that integrate with projects that the kids might be doing." Celia's library has also created a page called Countries of the World. One of the databases, CultureGrams, provides standard information about a country as well as cultural information. A database that many libraries have is Scholastic's Grolier Online, Lands and Peoples, which includes a feature called Culture Cross that compares the land, people, economy, and other features of various countries. "It also has a feature called Passport to Fun," Celia said, "that has some games and a quizmaster . . . a little lighter content."

Even though libraries have all these databases with accurate content, students and patrons primarily use Google. In response to this, Celia said, "We are trying to shift our gears so that we can blend and integrate databases with web resources to allow customers to search the way they want to, and in the process, help them to search Google successfully but with added value."

The challenge for librarians is to guide students to their student-oriented content while still giving control of the computer to the student. In the case of providing international texts, it may be even more vital to have an informed "guide on the side" so that students get to interact with texts they may never have considered in the past. "I verbally give them the tools," said Celia, "while I'm standing on the side, [letting them] do the discoveries themselves."

Teachers who are interested in teaching with a global emphasis should take advantage of their school and community libraries. Just taking a moment to send an email to a librarian requesting help to find texts with an international focus will probably result in a plethora of support. Of course, librarians also make themselves available to work with students directly, showing them ways to access international texts, but the first step should probably be for the teacher to consult with the librarian, who is often an untapped resource.

Creating Traveling Trunks

Celia also described kits that her library has put together that include items relating to certain cultures. Each kit (called Program in a Box) includes such items as recipes, books and stories, films, toys, and other items from a culture. For instance, in the Program in a Box for Japan, there is a candy sushi recipe, a story called "The Bet," and various other related items including posters and music CDs. This is similar to the "traveling trunks" that are created by such entities as the U.S. National Park Service (www.nps.gov/learn/trunks.htm) or museums (www.michenermuseum.org/teachers/trunk.php). The concept of traveling trunks could easily be expanded into a low-tech assignment; students could be assigned to fill a trunk with various artifacts related to a given culture. Students could use the Internet and library databases to research what items may be included in a traveling trunk as well as to find a rationale for why each item was included.

National Writing Project teacher consultant Karen Andrus Tollafield has created the following assignment, which requires students to create their own traveling trunks filled with actual and virtual artifacts.

Global Traveling Trunks
By Karen Andrus Tollafield

Overview

A great way to engage and motivate students is to make content come alive, especially when studying times and places far removed from the students' own world. One way to do this is through the use of traveling trunks. These are portable vessels containing artifacts relevant to the content, allowing teachers to bridge that global divide. These trunks can be created by teachers or students using in-person, hands-on items or the virtual world. Their purpose is both to learn more about another country and culture and to entice others to learn more about it.

Basic Premise

A hands-on learning experience promotes student investment in the content. Traveling trunks can be boxes, bags, baskets, suitcases, or any containers that can hold artifacts that are related to the content area under study. (These trunks are primarily used for bringing the world to the students, but they can even be used with autobiographical units as students open their trunks to reveal items that have personal meaning and bring their world to others.)

Students create global traveling trunks as individuals or in small groups. Some traveling trunks can be found in museums and libraries and may be available to teachers on loan. However, most of these relate to local and American history; this project goes one step further in taking the students to other countries and cultures. A couple of resources that demonstrate how ready-made traveling trunks are used are the National Park Service (n.d.; www.nps.gov/gett/forteachers /upload/Travel%20Trunk%20Guide.pdf) and the Kansas Historical Society (2012; www.kshs.org/p /traveling-resource-trunks/14969).

Creating their own traveling trunks will provide an authentic learning experience for your students as they do the research. You may need to procure parental permission since this project does involve Internet research.

Content

Traveling trunks can be used in any specific content area or as part of a cross-curricular unit. History (world, American, and local), geography, language arts, math, and science are all subjects that lend themselves to such a project. For example:

- Reading/language arts—Students learn more about the setting (place and time) and the characters of a story they are reading or writing about

- Social studies—Students learn about the history, culture, and geography of places they are studying

- Math, music, visual arts, physical education—Students learn more about the history and culture of various mathematicians, musicians and music, artists and works of art, and athletes and sports

Definition

Artifacts are usually considered to be objects of historical interest that show human workmanship, but you can adapt the definition to fit your needs. For instance, if you are going to use traveling trunks as part of a biographical/autobiographical unit of study, artifacts can be items with particular meaning to that person. If you are going to use traveling trunks as a virtual project or if students are not able to procure actual items, the students will need to use images of artifacts. Students could also use a mixture of real and virtual world items.

Format

Traveling trunks can be created by the teacher if there isn't adequate time for the students to create their own. The teacher chooses artifacts from the time period being studied and uses them in various ways:

- Simply as a visual aid or teaching tool in a whole-group setting
- As an individual hands-on center
- As assignments; artifacts are assigned to individuals or groups to research and share with the whole group at a later time

Ideally, traveling trunks are created by students (individually or in groups) as a research project and shared with the whole group.

Possible Culminating Project

Trunk exhibition: Each trunk is displayed in a living museum format in different rooms or in a larger multipurpose area. The students display their trunks and give a brief presentation about their artifacts as invited guests (parents, other classes, administrators, and such) rotate through each display.

Assessment

A checklist is provided as a framework, but you can easily adapt it for your needs or create a rubric if you prefer. This project is also a perfect vehicle for student input for the requirements and possible optional elements.

The Global Traveling Trunk Project

Project

You will create a global traveling trunk. Your goal is to collect items that are relevant to your chosen topic (country, culture, historical figure from another country or culture).

Procedure

1. Working alone or in small groups, you will choose a country, culture, or person you wish to learn more about.

2. You will conduct online research using sources from the provided list or other preapproved sites. You will be looking for as many of the following items that apply to your situation:

   - Map of location
   - Clothing worn

Continued→

- Music
- Items used (for daily work, play, and anything relevant to their particular culture and time period)

3. You will obtain or make as many artifacts (items from the preceding list) as you can for inclusion in your traveling trunk. You will eventually be displaying these items and presenting them. You should number each item and make a numbered list with brief descriptions of what each item is, its importance, and how it was used.

4. Keep in mind:

   - You want to make your trunk as attractive as possible. When choosing your vessel, think about what might work best for your particular items. A futuristic container is not appropriate for historical artifacts.

   - If you cannot obtain actual items, you will need to find photographs of the items for inclusion in your trunk.

   - You can find examples of the music online and play it via the computer or an iPod (or some other creative way—if you play an instrument yourself, perhaps).

5. You will display and present your trunk to the class and, possibly, in a traveling trunk exhibition for parents, other classes and teachers, and other various invited guests.

Checklist

The following checklist contains the elements on which your traveling trunk will be graded.

The trunk and items (overall look of display):

- ☐ The display is attractive and inviting (aesthetically pleasing), including the use of space.

- ☐ Any text (labeling of items) is written in a clear, easy-to-read font.

- ☐ If audio is used, it enhances the experience for the site visitor.

Content:

- ☐ Artifacts are relevant to the purpose.

- ☐ The content is comprehensive in scope (no glaring omissions of information).

Language (during presentation):

- ☐ Information is communicated clearly and effectively.

Conventions:

- ☐ Typewritten text is spelled, capitalized, and punctuated correctly.

Reading News of the World

The teacher who is interested in globalizing his or her classroom should have the students read the newspaper, according to noted media educator Frank W. Baker. Frank suggests putting an emphasis on international news as a relatively simple way to globalize a classroom. Helping students to deconstruct the news is a key function of the classic media literacy spin on global education. David Buckingham (2003) defines *media education* as "the process of teaching and learning about media" and *media literacy* as "the outcome—the knowledge and skills learners acquire" (p. 4). Equipping students with this kind of media literacy is crucial in the quest to help them become global digital citizens and interculturally critically literate (Myers & Eberfors, 2010). The Common Core State Standards mention the need for students to be able to "integrate and evaluate multiple sources of information presented in diverse formats and media (e.g., visually, quantitatively, as well as in words) in order to address a question or solve a problem" (NGA & CCSSO, 2010).

In his presentations to teachers across the country, Frank often advocates for the importance of global education and the important role media literacy education plays. "When you look at the definition of 21st century skills, global knowledge is embedded in everyone's definition," Baker pointed out. "Our students sometimes have blinders on and are not always aware of what's happening halfway around the world."

Technology has made the local newspaper available to anyone with the Internet, and looking at how the news is covered across the globe is a great way to introduce students to international perspectives. Frank encourages both teachers and students to become users of English language news sources originating overseas, such as Channel NewsAsia (www.channelnewsasia.com) or RT from Russia (http://rt.com) or Ireland's RTÉ (www.rte.ie), as well as the International Herald Tribune (http://global.nytimes.com/?iht), which originates in the United States as part of the *New York Times* but provides an international perspective. (Visit **go.solution-tree.com/21stcenturyskills** to access live links to the websites in this book.)

Frank suggests starting with a rather simple yet important activity in which students compare and contrast news coverage about a specific event as found in various news outlets from around the world. Students take one current event and compare and contrast the first sentence (known in journalism as the *lede*) in stories from different international sources covering the same event. "What information might be included in one version that's left out of another version?" is a question Frank said should be asked. To find multiple stories, Frank suggested using Google News (http://news.google.com), which allows the user to search for multiple stories internationally that are covering the same event or topic.

Comparing and Contrasting News Stories Across Media
By Frank W. Baker (Media Literacy Clearinghouse, www.frankwbaker.com)

Have students answer the following questions.

1. Where did you locate this news story?

    - Online (provide URL)

    - Social media (blog, tweet, or other source)

    - Domestic or international source

    - Broadcast (name of radio or television source and title of program)

    - Cable news outlet (name of cable network and title of program)

    - Newspaper (name of publication)

    - News magazine (name of publication)

2. What are the strengths (and possible weaknesses) of the different media? (The students should be familiar with all of the sources listed in #1 above.)

    This particular question revolves around the media literacy concept: form and content are closely related. So, for example, a five-minute newscast at the top of the hour on radio is more likely to contain many stories of shorter lengths; whereas a TV news magazine (such as *60 Minutes*, *Nightline*, and *Dateline*) is likely to spend more time covering a story.

3. Choosing one or two versions of the same news story (from different media), take note of the following:

    - What is the same in both versions?

    - What is different in both versions?

    - Who is quoted?

    - How many quotes are from male sources, female sources?

    - Considering the medium, how does each story differ?

4. Is there any evidence of bias and/or stereotypes in the story? If so, identify them and explain your reasoning.

It's clear that the burden is on the news consumer to filter world events, as more and more news sources are increasingly available.

Frank stated, "Thomas Jefferson said the health of our democracy depends on an informed citizenry. A student who fails to be globally informed is one who will not be competitive in a 21st century economy . . . Things that happen thousands of miles away do have an impact on our daily lives if we're paying attention. We have to appreciate the fact that we're not an isolated nation . . . The international connection is always there."

Going Somewhere Without Going Anywhere

During our discussion, Celia mentioned Global Trek (http://teacher.scholastic .com/activities/globaltrek), a website that helps teachers plan virtual field trips. This made me think of a book I read when a small boy, *Henry 3* (Krumgold, 1970), in which two boys get access to an old junked car, pretend that they are able to drive it, and go on elaborate imaginary trips using some maps and books that they bring along. Many teachers are currently assigning such make-believe trips for their students and find that, thanks to the Internet, these fake trips become almost as educational as if they were actual trips.

Garth Holman, seventh-grade social studies teacher at Beachwood Middle School in Cleveland, told me about a virtual trip project that he and his students built around a real person from Europe who had visited Beachwood Middle School when she was in the United States. This woman, named Estelle, was originally from France but had recently moved to Stockholm. Garth demonstrated to his students how they could use Google Earth (www.google.com/earth) to examine the places in this woman's life, even down to the street level.

Using Google Earth to pinpoint specific locations in Estelle's life, the students began to learn much about her current location, Stockholm, including that the city is made up of fifty islands. "We talked about peninsulas and archipelagos," said Garth. "Then we looked at old Stockholm and how we know that's the old Stockholm versus the new [Stockholm]." Moving beyond geographical features of the places they "visited," Garth and his students found the bakery and meat shop where Estelle shops as well as her home and workplace. They also looked at architecture via Google Earth, determining, for example, how certain sports stadia are based on ancient principles of design and structure.

Google Earth Activities
By Garth Holman

Use the following activity to inspire your own Google Earth adventure.

How Do I Use Google Earth?

1. Open Google Earth: www.google.com/earth

2. Under "View," make sure the following are turned on: Toolbar, Sidebar, Status bar, Show Navigation (always).

3. Make sure the following are checked:

   a. Border and labels

   b. Photos

   c. 3D buildings

   d. Oceans (only explore the Ocean, turn all other options off)

   e. Gallery (only check 360 cities, Ancient Rome, National Geographic magazine, and YouTube)

   f. More (only check Wikipedia)

4. To take a screenshot, press the "Prnt Scrn" button key (this may be different depending on your computer and operating system). This will take a shot of where you are. Build a table to put your images into.

5. Pick the Pushpin and rename it to tag places. This will be saved in your account.

6. Find the following and take a screenshot:

   a. Our school

   b. Your house

   c. Downtown Cleveland

   d. New York City

   e. Dubai and the tallest building in the world (view a YouTube video of the tallest building in the world)

   f. If you have time, you can find anything else you want.

Homework

Estelle will be visiting us for a few days. She is from France but currently lives and teaches in Stockholm, Sweden. She will have you use Google Earth tomorrow. What are three open-ended questions you would like to ask her?

How could Google Earth help you learn history?

What would be the benefit of using Google Earth in this classroom?

Quiz

For each, tag the place and take a screenshot.

- New Orleans (skyline)

- Chicago (skyline from the lake)

- Canterbury Cathedral (two images, one from above and one from the side)

Questions to Consider

1. Go back and look at the streets of Paris and Stockholm. How are they different and similar to each other (create a good list)?

2. Go back to Dubai and compare that landscape to Paris and Stockholm. How does it impact how the buildings are built?

3. How can the colors in Google Earth help you understand what you are seeing?

4. What is an archipelago? Where did we see an archipelago? What is a peninsula, and what country is a peninsula?

5. What inferences can you make about European culture from this Google Earth tour?

Estelle Visits—Google Earth It

For two days, Estelle will be visiting us from Europe. She is currently working on a PhD in geography at Stockholm University. We will be visiting part of her trip to Ohio in Google Earth.

1. Start with where Estelle went to college in Paris: 145 rue Saint-Dominique, Paris7

    a. Go to street view. What are the colors of the door?

    b. Look around. What is the very famous landmark in the area? Take a picture and save it.

2. Next stop, Jardin du Luxembourg. Find the Panthéon. Go to it and look at the monuments around the building. Get one picture and save it.

    a. How old do you think the buildings are in the area?

3. Now go to Swedenborgsgatan 4B, Stockholm. (Estelle will show you her window.)

    a. Zoom out. What is the special physical geography of Stockholm? Add a picture.

    b. How do you think this impacts the life of people in Stockholm?

    c. Zoom in. What is the name of the metro station at the corner of the street?

4. Next visit Gamla stan. Find the 360 view of Montelius Vägen (southwest) and take a picture.

5. We're off to a conference in London. Find Heathrow Airport (largest airport in the world), and get an image of it.

    a. The conference is at Imperial College. Find Albert Hall, a big round building hosting concerts, and take a picture in street view.

6. We enter the United States in Boston, Massachusetts. Take a picture of Logan Airport.

7. Head to a wedding around Hanover, New Hampshire. What is the name of the college in that town? Take a picture of the campus.

8. Take a bus back to Boston, then fly to Akron-Canton Airport. Get a picture.

While Garth takes his seventh graders on virtual field trips, he is also helping them get in touch with the international cultures that are in the overseas neighborhoods they are visiting.

Becoming a Historian in Your Own Backyard

To help students begin to think and act like historians, Garth has his students interview local people who spent their seventh-grade years in countries other than the United States. The students are to focus the inquiry around the question, What was seventh grade like for you? Students are expected to collect artifacts—such as yearbooks, report cards, photographs from middle school years, and even objects such as model cars or art projects—from their interview subjects. Documents are scanned and made a part of the students' final reports.

There are many Korean, European, and Russian émigrés living in Garth's district, and the interviews that the students do with them trigger many interesting stories. (Students are also allowed to conduct an interview over the phone or Skype if they can't find an appropriate and willing subject in town.) Garth said that the students "ultimately compare the world their parents lived in to the one today. Why is it that the pictures of their parents are in black and white? [What were the] meals they're eating? They're learning what a true historian has to do."

Garth said that this project and others like it "allow students to see cultural diffusion. As they interview people, the students naturally compare and contrast what they are hearing, seeing, and reading with their personal experiences. Similarities help students understand their global consecutiveness, even if their concept of the world ends at the driveway." Finding differences is an important part of the learning as well, reported Garth, as students begin to ask questions such as: "Why was it that way for them but not me?" and "Why can't it be like that for me?"

Seventh-Grade Interview Project
By Garth Holman

Goals for This Project

To think about:

- What is a historian, and what does he or she do?
- How has life changed since the interviewee was in school?

What Was Seventh Grade Like: Setting the Groundwork

1. Who are you planning to research and learn about?

2. What year did he or she graduate from high school?

3. When would the person have been in middle school, then?

4. Do a general search of the time period when your subject was in seventh grade. Write ten to twenty general facts about the time period (save the links)—for example, time lines; key international, national, or local events; presidents; music; TV; sports; and so on.

5. Try to get some artifacts from your interviewee's seventh-grade life, such as a yearbook, pictures, report cards, letters, crafts, advertisements from that era, and/or newspapers.

Interview Questions

School

Who was your favorite teacher, and why?

Explain the worst trouble you got in.

What were school lunches like, and how much were they?

Home

What type of work did you have to do at home?

What was your first job, and how did you feel about it?

How did the economy impact your life (recession or boom)?

How did your family get around? What was your first car?

How did your parents discipline you?

Tell me about your relationship in your family.

Social Life

Why did you have the friends that you had?

What inspired or influenced you as a child?

What did you want to be when you grew up, and what did you do to achieve it?

How have prices changed since you were in school?

Current Events

What tragic events occurred, and how did they impact you?

Student-Created Textbooks

Garth and his students take much of their work and use it to create their own student-created textbook focusing on world history (http://dgh.wikispaces.com).

The idea for this textbook project was developed several years ago by Garth and his then student teacher, Mike Pennington. The first venue for the homemade textbook was Wikibooks (www.wikibooks.org). Students were assigned a standard from the social studies curriculum and were expected to create a wiki based on that standard. "We got a couple paragraphs with some info about a topic," Garth reported.

The students wrote more extensively during the second year, and in the third year, the project was transferred to Wikispaces (www.wikispaces.com). Garth explained that they found Wikibooks somewhat more difficult to use than Wikispaces, but, candidly, he admitted the root cause for switching to Wikispaces: when he came back for the next school year, he could not remember the password for his Wikibooks account.

The second year, students started scanning in political cartoons and other texts such as Prezis (Prezi is a presentational tool, similar to PowerPoint, and a presentation that is composed using Prezi is often referred to as *a Prezi*). As of this writing, hundreds of students are involved with writing, editing, and maintaining the textbook between Garth's students and Mike's students at Chardon Middle School. Garth and Mike increasingly realized that they had some copyright issues and showed the students how to use Creative Commons (http://creativecommons .org). Diagrams and illustrations that couldn't be found online or couldn't be used due to copyright were created by the students themselves. "We had a kid who was so good at iMovie," Garth reported, "he proceeded to make movies for every topic we studied. It became a great avenue for learning." Garth knows of at least three districts that are using the student-created textbook, and Alan November has profiled the project in one of his IdeaJams (Elmer, 2011; http://engage.intel.com /thread/4548).

Garth feels that the textbook project has internationalized his students: "The fact that kids thirty-five miles apart are engaged in writing a textbook on the Internet for the world to view is the first phase of a real global education. They have to have a new perspective of how they write and how others in their audience will perceive the material. With thousands of international hits on this textbook, students are making global connections each and every day. As time moves forward, we hope to find a school to write a parallel version of the book to show how culture impacts historical memory."

Garth has many ideas for continuing to internationalize his classroom, including conducting interviews with experts on the topics being studied. For instance, he already has some experts lined up for the students to interview on the topic of the Black Death. These interviews will be preserved as podcasts and stored on one of the pages of the class textbook that will include various other related material such as political cartoons, video clips, and printed texts. He also wants to find a school in Western Europe that will create its own textbook, with pages that mirror his classroom's, on such topics as the Reformation, feudalism, or gothic architecture, from their perspective. "Kids are bright," Garth said. "Nobody listens. This gives them a platform to have an audience."

Other Ideas for Virtual Field Trips
By Karen Andrus Tollafield

Imagine being able to take your students on a trip to visit the pyramids of Egypt or dive under the ocean searching for shipwrecks. Field trips can be wonderful opportunities for students to gain firsthand knowledge related to various concepts being studied, and with the help of technology, you can go just about anywhere! Virtual field trips can be the next best thing to actually being there. Luckily, resources are available at all levels, from ready-made adventures to student-created explorations. Following are resources for finding lesson plans with ready-made field trips and tips on creating your own. Primarily, however, you will learn how to guide your students through the creation of their own versions of virtual field trips we will call "travel wikis."

Ready-Made Virtual Field Trips

For teachers who don't have much class time to devote to the preparation and creation of a virtual field trip, there are many sites available for just about every content area. Following are a few examples.

Basic

- WikiFieldTrip, www.wikifieldtrip.org—This site is prepared by and linked to Wikipedia. Basically, it offers a wide variety of places, landmarks, and some events. You can choose from a list of popular sites or type in your own in hopes it exists in the database. It starts with an aerial map of the location with points on which to click. These links take you to the Wikipedia page to give information.

- Inside the White House Interactive Tour, www.whitehouse.gov/about/interactive-tour—This site provides a tour of the White House.

Museums

- The Teacher's Guide Virtual Tours and Fieldtrips, www.theteachersguide.com/virtualtours .html#Museums—Here you will find a comprehensive list of various museum sites with interactive content.

Continued→

- The Art Institute of Chicago, www.artic.edu/aic—Provides various tours of exhibits.
- Smithsonian, www.si.edu/Exhibitions/Search/Virtual—This site offers a wide variety of exhibitions from the Smithsonian.
- WebExhibits, www.webexhibits.org—This site provides an excellent interactive museum of science, humanities, and culture.

Adventures

- Google Earth, www.googleearth.com—This is a comprehensive site that allows one to locate both famous and not-so-famous geographical locations around the world.
- Interactive Tour of the Solar System, http://nineplanets.org/tour—This site offers an up-close visit to our solar system.
- PBS, www.pbs.org/wgbh/nova/adventures—PBS offers a comprehensive list of adventures from around the world.
- 4-H Virtual Farm, www.sites.ext.vt.edu/virtualfarm—Here you can visit a 4-H farm.
- Colonial Williamsburg, www.history.org—Visit Colonial Williamsburg through this site.
- Natural Wonders of the World Field Trip, www.field-guides.com/sci/natwon/index.htm—Here you can discover the seven natural wonders of the world up close.

Teacher-Prepared Virtual Field Trips

For teachers who want to create their own virtual trips, the following sites may be helpful. Simply visiting some of the ready-made sites will also provide a variety of ideas using platforms with which you may be comfortable. Creating your own virtual trips allows you to control the content and tailor the modules to your students' needs. Three of the many available sites are:

- TrackStar, http://trackstar.4teachers.org/trackstar
- SimpleK12, http://simplek12.com/virtualfieldtripfreepackage
- Rick Steves' Smartphone Apps for Travelers, www.ricksteves.com/plan/tips/apps.htm

Helpful Tips for Ready-Made or Teacher-Created Trips

- These virtual field trips can be used as individual or small-group activities, but you may consider projecting the site on a screen and taking the tour as a whole class.
- Teach an introductory lesson prior to the trip.
- Consider using some type of written question guide for students to follow as they take their tour so they have a particular purpose on which to focus as they navigate the website.
- Provide a follow-up activity.

Overview

Students will create a travel wiki as individuals or in small groups. There are many different wiki websites that are free and easy to use. We like using wikis for their user-friendly format and ease of collaboration. You may need to procure parental permission since this project does involve Internet research. Also be sure to familiarize yourself with the list of research sites provided here prior to allowing students access to them.

Purpose

To learn more about another location and to entice others to learn more about it

Curricular Tie-Ins

(You can easily adapt the project to reflect the content you wish to cover.)

- Reading or language arts: Learn more about the setting of a story (either reading or writing).
- Social studies: Learn about the history, culture, and geography of places you are studying.
- Math, music, visual arts, and physical education: Learn more about the history and culture of various mathematicians, musicians and music, artists and works of art, and athletes and sports.

Assessment

A checklist is provided as a framework, but you can easily adapt it for your needs or create a rubric if you prefer. This project is also a perfect vehicle for student input into the requirements and possible optional elements.

The Travel Wiki Project

Project

You will create a travel wiki. Pretend that you are working for the travel bureau of a particular place and your job is to create an interactive site to persuade travelers to visit. The more attractive and complete your wiki, the more enticing it will be.

Procedure

1. Working alone or in small groups, you will choose a travel destination.
2. You will conduct online research using sources from the provided list or other preapproved sites. You will be looking for as many of the following features as apply to your situation:
   - Map with location highlighted
   - Major cities pinpointed
   - Regions
   - Weather, seasons
   - Historic sites and landmarks
   - Scenic attractions
   - Tourist attractions
   - Cultural attractions (for example, museums)
   - Entertainment (such as plays, concerts, and sports)
   - Recreational activities (fun things to do for the whole family)
   - Language (or languages) spoken (include a few helpful phrases)
   - Currency with exchange rates
   - Cuisine (food for which the area is known), restaurants, and marketplaces

Continued→

- Major religions, places of worship
- Holidays
- Accommodations (hotels) available with approximate costs
- Resorts, cruises
- Tours available and group rates
- Transportation (to and from and what types available while visiting)

3. Keep in mind, you want to make your wiki as attractive and user-friendly as possible. Include:

- Photos, graphics, maps, and possibly videos
- Text in a clear, easy-to-read font
- Wiki pages arranged in some kind of logical order so site visitors can easily find what they're looking for

4. You will also want to decide whether or not you will use audio on your site. Consider:

- Narration of text
- Use of sounds to enhance your site (for example, if you have a photo of the ocean, you may want to include seagull sounds to help your visitors feel as if they are standing on that beach)

Resources for Research

The following are approved websites for your research. If you know of others, please get preapproval before use.

- www.travel.nettop20.com (includes list of popular travel resource sites)
- www.travel.yahoo.com
- www.fodors.com
- www.lonelyplanet.com
- www.frommers.com
- www.tripadvisor.com
- www.virtualtourist.com
- www.concierge.com

Checklist

The following checklist contains the elements on which your travel wiki will be graded.

Design of the site (overall layout):

- ☐ The display is attractive and inviting (aesthetically pleasing), including use of space, colors, and readability.
- ☐ There is a balance of appropriate photos, graphics, and text that enhance the content and create interest.
- ☐ The text is written in a clear, easy-to-read font with various sizes appropriate for headings.

- [ ] There is a logical organization and consistent formatting from page to page.
- [ ] It is easy to navigate.
- [ ] If audio is used, it enhances the experience for the site visitor.

Content:

- [ ] Information is relevant to the purpose.
- [ ] The content is comprehensive in scope (no glaring omissions of information).

Language:

- [ ] Information is communicated clearly and effectively.
- [ ] If audio is used, the speaker is clear and grammatically correct.

Conventions:

- [ ] Typewritten text is spelled, capitalized, and punctuated correctly.

Internationalizing the Curriculum

Another way to incorporate a global education is to use an international curriculum, such as the International Baccalaureate (IB; www.ibo.org), which is used by over 3,000 schools in over 140 countries. There are three different levels of curricula: one for early childhood, one for middle childhood, and one for high school. The IB was brought up in many interviews for this book and is an immense force for standardizing curriculum on a global level.

According to its website (IB, 2012), the organization "aims to develop inquiring, knowledgeable, and caring young people who help to create a better and more peaceful world through intercultural understanding and respect." Founded in 1968, the organization now features a curriculum with six main categories: (1) studies in language and literature, (2) language acquisition, (3) individuals and society, (4) experimental sciences, (5) mathematics and computer science, and (6) the arts. Although individual schools are permitted to tailor lessons, somewhat, to local circumstances, the standardization of the curriculum worldwide makes it unique as an international curriculum. If the IB student passes the exams related to the curriculum, the resulting diploma is recognized by universities all over the world.

According to its website, the IB Diploma Programme is in place in 3,397 high schools all over the world including 774 in the United States and 148 high schools in Canada, making it a premier worldwide curriculum. One of the schools happens to be my alma mater, Firestone High School, in Akron, Ohio. I talked with Judith Harrison, IB coordinator at Firestone, to find out what the IB looks like at ground level. The IB has been in existence at Firestone for several years and has succeeded in this urban school of approximately 1,300 students with a racial makeup of 52 percent black, 41 percent white, and 4 percent multiracial. Approximately 43 percent of Firestone's students are categorized as economically disadvantaged.

Judith recounted how the IB came to be at Firestone: "In 1995, after a year-long application process, including a site visitation, Firestone was selected to join the International Baccalaureate Organization (IBO) as an IB World School. The first graduating class in 1998 consisted of twenty students. Since then, nearly 400 students have completed the two-year curriculum."

Judith pointed out that students from many diverse neighborhoods take part in the IB program and do well. She said, "Our admission policy is not based solely on test scores and other achievement measures but rather a number of factors including student commitment. The program reflects the cultural diversity of our community. Applications by low-income and minority students have grown over the fifteen years of our program, and our acceptance rate is inclusive."

Judith tells the story of a black male from a single-parent family, eligible for lunch subsidy: "This IB student was one of our valedictorians and is currently at the top of the class in medical school. Without the rigor of the IB curriculum, it is highly debatable if he would have had the necessary preparation for admission and successful completion of a medical program." In fact, Judith reported that graduates of the IB program at Firestone are now studying at universities such as Harvard, MIT, Brown, Yale, Stanford, Northwestern, and Bryn Mawr.

Judith teaches a course called the Theory of Knowledge, which is a course specific to the IB curriculum. The course is designed to elicit critical thinking about knowledge itself, as students grapple with questions such as: What counts as knowledge? How does it grow? What are its limits? Who owns knowledge? What is the value of knowledge? and What are the implications of having or not having knowledge?

She said, "I would argue that my own teaching has been enhanced by the IB curriculum. Specifically, the Theory of Knowledge course allows students' experiences across academic disciplines to inform their understanding of the world. Internationalism is fostered by an examination of significant knowledge issues through multiple points of view. Membership in the IBO presents frequent opportunities for professional development through training, teacher forums, and collaboration with faculty at other member schools."

In addition to the IB program, other curriculum models for internationalizing the curriculum are available for educators interested in making changes that permeate the entire school. The Asia Society's International Studies Schools Network (http://asiasociety.org/education/international-studies-schools-network) and the New Tech Network (www.newtechnetwork.org) are two popular resources for adding a global emphasis to a classroom or an entire school. Another example is Deeper Learning, part of the William and Flora Hewlett Foundation (www .hewlett.org/programs/education-program/deeper-learning).

If a school district doesn't want to devote an entire school's focus to global education, it will sometimes create a school within a school, offering such specialized elements as foreign language instruction, service learning, and travel opportunities. Many of these specialized curricula feature a project-based approach in which students work on interdisciplinary goals that often involve international collaboration.

As I spoke with teachers who were taking first steps to internationalize their classrooms, I noticed that it didn't take long before they had made an attempt to reach out and communicate and collaborate with teachers and students on an international level. These kinds of "flat classroom" projects will be the focus of the next chapter.

The World Across Classrooms

Oh, the places you'll go!

Dr. Seuss

In the previous chapter, we discussed taking the first steps toward globalizing a classroom. In this chapter, we will look at strategies for taking the next steps and beginning to reach out to classrooms both down the hall and across the world. Perhaps inspired by the popular books published on the topic (Friedman, 2005; Pink, 2005) or the increasing prevalence of broadband Internet connectivity, teachers are showing an increasing interest in reaching beyond the classroom walls and connecting with those a half a world away. And, as you will see by looking at the work of teachers described in this chapter, it is quite easy to do. You will hear teachers describe the powerful results such communications and collaborations have for their students.

There are several ways to connect with faraway schools. Some teachers use email (Borsheim, 2004), but most use various online discussion forums such as message boards, wikis, and Nings (Beeghly, 2005; Hathaway, 2011; Larson, 2009; Richard, 2011; Scharber, 2009). A Ning is a social network that one may create at a specific website (www.ning.com). Ning started in 2005 as a free resource but now is fee-based. Regardless of the platform, a trend in global collaborations is setting up common virtual work spaces for students to work together on various projects (Hull, Stornaiuolo, & Sahni, 2010; Maltese & Naughter, 2010; Paris, 2010) or to foster intercultural critical literacy (Myers & Eberfors, 2010). In this chapter, teachers who have worked to set up these kinds of international collaborations will share specific examples in detail, complete with depictions of all the challenges, logistics, and payoffs involved.

Foreign Language Education

In conducting the research for this book, I was surprised that little was mentioned about the foreign language elements that must be related to international collaborations. Perhaps this is because English is so commonly spoken across the world—many of the teachers I spoke with conduct their collaborations in English even if their collaborations are with non-English-speaking countries.

Having been a curriculum supervisor assigned to work with foreign language teachers, I know of the great work that these teachers have done to foster intercultural understanding and the unsung lead that they have often taken in global education. Indeed, teaching for this kind of international understanding is woven into the National Standards for Foreign Language Education (American Council on the Teaching of Foreign Languages, n.d.). At the same time, new technologies provide new and engaging ways for students to learn a foreign language.

Chad Everett Allan is a former South Carolina Spanish Teacher of the Year runner-up and is now teaching Spanish at Kent State University while pursuing doctoral studies. Chad encourages the use of Twitter, YouTube, and Skype to help his students with some of the basics they need when communicating with someone in Spanish.

He is vocal about the key component that global education should play in the foreign language classroom: "We are well past simply having a classroom where our students are drilling verbs, filling in blanks with random vocabulary, rehearsing dialogues, and true-falsing cultural knowledge to death. . . . Global education provides [a reason] for our students to communicate in the target language, compare their own culture with another as a process of learning, and . . . connect with real opportunities to speak and experience 'self' through communication."

Excited about what technology has brought to the foreign language classroom, Chad provides examples of how new media may be used not only to give students experience in speaking a foreign language but also to achieve some level of global and self-awareness.

Using New Media to Learn Spanish
By Chad Everett Allan

This project serves several purposes and should be viewed as a journey of learning with the assumption that not all learners will move through the same route or at the same rate in learning the target language or the applications of current socio-media or technology. The idea comes from recognizing the importance of producing better students and citizens who can participate fully in the world around them by exposing them to new views of literacy and learning using tools that connect them to their daily lives and a global community.

This extension project is designed for learners who might travel to a Spanish-speaking country and implements tasks for all types of learners as it pertains to their health, health needs, medical attention, and communicating about general health ideas and issues. The more students can connect to authentic sources and a more global view of learning, the more they will want to engage in and actively create and explore sources that are a part of their "real" daily life.

The overall project approaches, meets, and exceeds multiple national and state standards for technology, communication, comparing cultures, connecting, and global learning.

Good Health Abroad

The first task of this project involves visiting an online avatar doctor who will answer your questions, but only if you speak in Spanish!

Task One

1. Click the image of the doctor and continue on to the conversation starter.

   The student will engage with an avatar doctor and have a sense of what questions would generally be asked prior to and during a doctor's visit. By clicking on the image, students are taken to a web page to create a preassessment by a patient that could be used to advise a doctor.

2. Once in the "starter," get a general idea of the information provided. Look at images, key words, and cognates, and transfer your knowledge and familiarity of the web page.

   Once the learner has clicked to the web page, he or she will view various images, questions, content, and prompting questions about general health, concerns, and preparations for a visit to a doctor. This connection to global health issues, language that is familiar and not familiar (but accessible via cognates and context), as well as general familiarity with health visits will allow the learner to review, decode, reflect, and begin to understand the context.

3. Continue through steps 1–4, following the prompts on the web page.

   The learner will follow the steps in the web page. The steps are:

Continued→

1. Select the themes, questions, and reminders that you want to include in your card that you will bring to visit the doctor. A list of themes is offered about different aspects of health and conditions for the learner to select from.

2. Click on the guide to initiate the conversation with the doctor.

3. Respond to the questions that you choose or see appropriate based on the themes that you have selected.

4. Print the guide so that you can bring it with you to your visit with the doctor.

5. After you have printed the guide, you will also want to save a copy in PDF and email it to your professor.

6. Discuss what you have found out prior to your visit with the doctor. This can be done via chat or email. How have you learned to assess your health and understand the relationship between health visits that you have in your culture and another culture? Can you compare and connect to some of these? Would you be prepared to visit and explain your needs, conditions, and concerns?

Task Two: Twitter Response 1

You have decided that after visiting the doctor and following his advice, it would be a good idea to offer some help to others who may have the same symptoms or concerns that you have.

1. Create a Twitter (www.twitter.com) account as the following: @MSMH+your last name+first letter of your first name. Do not use an account you already have.

2. Request to follow the teacher's Twitter account at @mesientomalhoy.

3. Once you are accepted, the teacher will post three tweets describing how he is feeling on any given day. Read the tweets and any responses that have been posted previously.

4. You will need to respond in full sentences to those tweets in Spanish, giving advice to help your teacher feel better. These recommendations and suggestions should not repeat the advice given in previous tweets. Be creative! Can you think of regional or cultural remedies that you know of that were used in your family when you were not feeling well? Put yourself in that scenario. Remember, you are limited to 140 characters.

Task Three: Twitter Response 2

Living abroad can be difficult in many ways, and staying healthy is key. You want to help students find equilibrium in their student lives as well as have much better health.

1. From his Twitter account at @mesientomalhoy, your teacher will be sharing three tweets giving scenarios in which people are looking for advice after getting into a bad situation or in a conflict dealing with making good decisions.

2. You will need to read the tweets and any responses that have been posted previously.

3. Respond in full sentences to two of those tweets in Spanish, giving advice. You should not repeat the advice given from previous tweets.

4. In addition to your tweets, you must supply a valuable resource for each tweet. These sources must be in a media form or a resource that you have created that can be linked and viewed online. Look for unique and valuable sources for exchange students living abroad, such as proper eating and exercise or whatever you think would be most valuable.

Task Four

Blog Discussion Board

Now that you have become more comfortable with your opinions and personal views of how to live a healthy and productive life while living abroad, it is time for you to express yourself in a more developed and complete way. You will participate in a discussion board to do just that.

1. Visit the discussion board. A series of questions have been provided, the answers to which will help you respond appropriately to the question, What do you do to live a healthy life? (¿Qué haces para vivir una vida sana?)

2. Review the questions and answer at least eight. Use those answers to create a complete response to the Spanish question in essay form.

3. Focus on using the appropriate register, creating cohesive content and fluid wording, making a thorough response, and promoting communication among bloggers, providing evidence of your understanding that blogs are global and thus accessed and viewed all over the world.

4. Prior to responding, you should review what others have written to avoid copying their work.

Note: You are not required to respond to the postings, but please feel free to do so.

Task Five

YouTube and My Opinion (Mi Opinión)

A large part of making global connections and understanding a foreign culture is exposure to current media and how others view the world. Reflect on what you see as a social or health problem related to relationships, health, sports, personal care, eating well, exercise, avoiding accidents, or anything else that is related to "good health" in your culture *and* the new culture that you are experiencing.

1. Search for appropriate explanatory (to some degree) videos that relate to what to do to live a good life or what not to do if you want to live a good life.

2. Present the video (or a portion of the video) to the class of other exchange students and give oral commentary about why you chose the video and how it relates to the class's discussions. You have lots of freedom in how you choose to approach the discussion. Be sure to test that the video will load when you present. You will have a minimum of five minutes to present. Of the five minutes, a minimum of three must be your original commentary. The presentation must also involve the audience and should engage them in open-ended questions.

3. Be creative and think outside the caja!

Furthering Your Language Practice

You have returned from your study abroad. The connections have only started! You have learned a new culture and a new language, and have made global connections that bring a greater appreciation for how we are all different and alike. You want to continue to grow in your abilities and knowledge by continuing to communicate. Students from all over the world are learning to speak English and about your culture just as you are learning to speak Spanish and explore the many Hispanic cultures.

Continued→

Task One: Practice (La Práctica)

You and a class partner need to create and exchange an ooVoo (www.oovoo.com), Skype (www .skype.com), or similar account. You will need to create a schedule to practice speaking with each other, becoming more familiar and relaxed with the process. Focus on how you are feeling, your likes, dislikes, family, friends, and tastes in music, art, and culture. The basic expectations for this conversation are:

- Greet your friend and engage.

- Inquire about how he or she is feeling.

- Exchange (asking and answering questions) related to your likes, dislikes, family, friends, pastimes, and tastes in music, art, and culture.

- Close the dialogue appropriately.

- The dialogue should be spontaneous and not rehearsed. New information should be exchanged each time you begin a new conversation.

- Ask and answer questions fully and appropriately.

- Focus on pronunciation to the best of your ability so that it is natural and does not interfere with comprehension.

- Make language use accurate and meaningful.

One of your video conversations should be recorded and emailed to the teacher's ooVoo or Skype account.

Basic Rubric

NR—Video was not submitted.

0—The conversation is irrelevant, weak, or an incomprehensible exchange between the participants.

1—The conversation is meaningful but limited, and no new information is exchanged.

2—The conversation is meaningful, and some new information is exchanged. Student is engaged and participates.

3—The conversation is meaningful with new information, and the student is engaged, participates fully, and shares openly.

Note: *Engaged* means that the speaker responds fully, asks questions, and reacts appropriately to the context.

Task Two: Connect

Lenguajero (www.lenguajero.com) and other similar sites provide learners with the opportunity to engage in communication with people in foreign countries. As an extension of your practice in and outside the classroom, this exercise allows you to make a *global connection* and to then share your experience with your classmates.

1. Create a Lenguajero account. Follow the instructions for setting up your account and establishing a connection.

2. Set a schedule for when you will be able to communicate with the global community.

3. Follow your schedule and keep a diary, visual board, memo set, or whatever you feel will help you discuss what you have learned in your communications with that community.

4. Consider the following questions: What are your interactions like? How often have you communicated? What do you learn about the target culture? What do you share about your own culture? What limitations are there? Where do you feel there are no limitations? Do you battle biases and/or prejudices? Have you realized something new? Do you communicate more in Spanish or English? Do you negotiate meaning in your communication?

5. Present a visual presentation of your new knowledge and how this connection will benefit you now and later in your life.

Task Three: Extension Project Reflection and Self-Critique

Nombre:

This is to be completed after your practices through Lenguajero and all other components of the project. This rubric is designed for reflection on your learning and the tasks that have been included in the project. Complete with commentary in the appropriate box.

Elements	Excellent/ Valuable	Very Good/ Good	Poor/Lacking
How would you describe your acquisition of new knowledge and ability based on the tasks completed in this project?			
Although some tasks are more difficult than others, how would you describe the tasks overall compared to what you were learning and expected to know from just the textbook?			
How would you describe your use of time given to practice and completing and submitting the work expected?			
How would you rate your appreciation of global connections and understanding a new culture while engaging in this project?			
Based on all of the collaborative and communicative activities, how would you describe your experience as a learner using social media, technology, and Web 2.0 applications to enhance your learning?			

Of course, an educator doesn't have to speak a foreign language or aspire to teach one in order to take part in the growing conversation about global education. A great way for a teacher to start the process of integrating global education into the classroom is to take part in an international discussion about education. Once a teacher has decided to jump into some kind of exploration of global education, there are many resources on the Internet and elsewhere available to do so.

The Global Education Conference

One of the most comprehensive sites, and a good place to start for any teacher interested in internationalizing the classroom, is the Global Education Collaborative (http://globaleducation.ning.com). Cofounders Lucy Gray and Steve Hargadon wanted to create an online space for people interested in global education. Within this Ning, the Global Education Conference happens each November with thousands of people taking part in live presentations that are also archived and freely accessible on an ongoing basis. The site remains a vibrant and fascinating online repository throughout the entire year for anyone who wants to learn and dialogue about this topic.

I spoke with Lucy about the genesis of the Global Education Conference. Concerned with how unconnected educators were, Lucy created the Global Education Collaborative, a "place where you can meet and develop collegial relationships. We have urgent problems that need to be addressed, and in order to work on these problems, we must connect globally." Steve approached Lucy, wanting to combine her community with his, Elluminate, now Blackboard Collaborate, to impact education in a significant way. Elluminate/Blackboard Collaborate (www.blackboard.com) is an online venue for teaching courses, providing staff development, or hosting meetings. Lucy remembered, "I suggested a virtual conference, and the event was born!"

Lucy and Steve had participated in the K–12 Online Conference (http://k12online conference.org) and thought it was a model they could emulate. According to Lucy, they ended up having 400 sessions in 2010 with "several conference strands, including one called Learning 2.0 for submissions that didn't fit into our definition of global education and that were more focused on general education."

Lucy and Steve remain committed to continuing the conference. Lucy believes that the benefits of participating in the Global Education Collaborative and

Conference are immeasurable to teachers and to their future students: "The Global Education Conference is an opportunity to partake in professional development at any time and virtually any place. Another benefit for participants is that they can choose sessions aligned to their interest and needs. In addition to networking opportunities, educators also interact with thought leaders in education and have a much more intimate experience than they would at a face-to-face conference. Presenting at the conference also gives educators an authentic audience and a chance to publicize projects and potentially find collaborators. For students, the same applies. If they present, they can find authentic, supportive audiences, spread the word about their work, and practice their communication skills."

The Flat Classroom Project

A well-known international classroom collaboration project is the Flat Classroom Project (www.flatclassroomproject.net) started by teachers Julie Lindsay and Vicki Davis. Julie teaches at an international school in Beijing, China. Vicki teaches in the Westwood Schools in Georgia. I spoke with Julie via Skype about her story and the start of the Flat Classroom Project.

Julie reminisced, "Vicki and I first interacted in the K–12 Online Conference in 2006. Vicki was running a session on how to collaborate globally using a wiki. That's the first time we connected. She was talking about reading *The World Is Flat* [Friedman, 2005], and I had a senior class, and we were doing the same. I left a comment on her blog: 'Here I am in Bangladesh—let's join our classes together.' We brainstormed. What tools are we going to use? I remember the Skype call where we brainstormed the name of the project: Flat World? Global Classroom? Until we came up with the Flat Classroom." As the project is described on the official Flat Classroom (n.d.) website, "One of the main goals of the project is to 'flatten' or lower the classroom walls so that instead of each class working isolated and alone, two or more classes are joined virtually to become one large classroom. This is done through the Internet using Web 2.0 tools such as Wikispaces and Ning."

The first Flat Classroom project went live on November 22, 2006, and lasted for about three weeks. From the beginning, there have been several components to the Flat Classroom Project for the students to work on, including a prescribed amount of time, usually a few weeks. The essence of the project is that the students get to collaborate with students across the world, looking at the trends that Friedman (2005) identifies in his book that have flattened our world (made us closer than ever to each other, in other words). As an outgrowth of studying these flattening elements, the students produce a product that serves to illuminate one of the flattening features. Julie explained, "The students not only have to do wiki collaboration, but they also have to create a personal multimedia artifact, and part of this is outsourced to another student not in the same class, probably across the world."

The students in the collaborating classrooms are divided up into eleven groups and assigned one of the forces that have flattened the world, according to Friedman:

Group 1: Connecting the World Online

Group 2: How the World Wide Web Has Changed the World

Group 3: How Work Flow Software Can Enhance Productivity and Communication

Group 4: The Changing Shape of Information

Group 5: Why We Should be Promoting Web 2.0 Tools for Sharing Information

Group 6: Globalization and Outsourcing

Group 7: Google Takes Over the World

Group 8: Personal Learning Environments and Social Networking

Group 9: Mobile and Ubiquitous

Group 10: Virtual Communication

Group 11: Wireless Connectivity (Flat Classroom, n.d.)

Students then begin to work on a wiki that includes information related to their flattening trend. As mentioned, ultimately, the students are to produce a multimedia artifact, part of which is outsourced to students working in another classroom.

Julie credits several projects for leading the way and making the Flat Classroom Project possible, including ePals (www.epals.com), Global SchoolNet (www .globalschoolnet.org), and International Schools CyberFair (www.globalschoolnet .org/gsncf). According to Julie, what they wanted was to "go beyond the wow—everyone loves that Skype call, but then you've got to take that excitement and build it into something more meaningful. . . . We get students together from different classrooms with ideas to change the world, and the next step is to try to get action plans implemented" in response to the flattening elements.

Julie and Vicki have created several spin-offs of the Flat Classroom Project. "The following year," said Julie, "we started the Horizon Project, based on the Horizon

Report of emerging technologies. . . . We got into collaboration with Don Tapscott and relaunched it as the NetGen Education Project in 2009. About 2007, we started Digiteen [in which students] explore different areas of digital citizenship and go back to their school communities and develop an action plan. It's very much Tom Friedman's idea about globalization but coming back and localizing the knowledge into an action plan. It's implemented and shared. We've got students using Edmodo and, if they are older, a Ning for that one. We use a Ning for Flat Classroom and NetGen Ed."

Another project that they designed, based on a student initiative at the first Flat Classroom Project in 2009 is Eracism (www.eracismproject.org), a global student debate project: "We created an asynchronous debate using VoiceThread, and classes would record their opening. Then it would go to the next class, and the teacher would listen to the recording, give them two minutes, and then they would respond. We got through all the elimination rounds and the final debate was held in a virtual world."

Julie is excited about a new project they've created for upper elementary students called A Week in the Life: "It's meant to be a documentation of a week in the life. Students, in mixed global teams, gather multimedia and prepare an artifact that can be used for conversation [about such topics as] the environment, holidays, food, and entertainment. The classrooms are meeting in Edmodo. We've got grades 3 through 5. They explore different Web 2.0 tools—VoiceThread, Glogster—and then with teachers' help, they create a final artifact and post it. . . . It's meant to be not just a show and tell, but to gather media and put it together so that it's saying something significant."

Even though Vicki and Julie only see each other twice a year in person, they talk constantly and continue to advocate strongly for the kind of teaching that they see as necessary. They are resolute that the practice students get working on the Flat Classroom Project is necessary to prepare them for a life in which "they will have to know how to work with other people when they aren't face to face with them. They'll have to know how to conduct a Skype call, know how to get into a 3-D world, and know how to use a chat room window and how to communicate asynchronously. . . . By having to interact, converse, or create products together, students learn more about the life and culture of their team partners than they would from a humanities book or from the media. Through this enhanced global awareness and experiential learning, they break through stereotypes and banish ethnocentricity and, we hope, realize that differences make us stronger and can make the world a better place."

Teachers who are interested in setting up these kinds of international collaborations can explore the following sources for international classroom collaborations:

- ePals Global Community, www.epals.com
- Flat Classroom Projects, http://flatclassroomproject.net
- Global Education Conference, http://globaleducation.ning.com
- Global Nomads Group, http://gng.org
- Global SchoolNet, www.globalschoolnet.org
- iEARN, www.iearn.org
- SchoolsOnline, http://schoolsonline.britishcouncil.org/home
- TakingITGlobal, www.tigweb.org/about

Setting Up Your Own International Collaborations

Clarence Fisher is a middle school English and social studies teacher in rural Manitoba, in a town called Snow Lake. Although his students and their families have to drive for six hours to reach the nearest shopping mall, they are just a mouse click away from students across the world with whom they collaborate. Clarence teaches at the Joseph H. Kerr School, a K–12 school with only several hundred students. After traveling extensively overseas and teaching in an international school, Clarence returned to Snow Lake with one of his goals being to bring the world to his students, thus Clarence and his students have taken part in several international collaborations.

One of the first international collaborations that Clarence set up was with the help of an organization called International Teen Life, using the organization's projects as a template for his own project (http://internationalteenlife.pbworks .com). The collaboration included his classroom, one in the United States, one in Colombia, and one in Indonesia.

Clarence described how he usually begins an international collaboration project: "I make up an iGoogle page and usually start with between seven and nine feeds. I find stuff that I'm interested in, some tech stuff, some science stuff. I try to find hot blogs where there are issues going on. For instance, we used to use a blog called Nata village (http://natavillage.typepad.com). It was kept by two nurses in Africa who had full-blown HIV and wrote about that experience. I would set up all the feeds, and I would share it with all the kids in my class."

Another early step in Clarence's international collaboration projects involves teaching his students how to use Global Voices (http://globalvoicesonline.org) to select a country and subscribe to that feed. "I call it required reading," said Clarence. "One thing I make them do during the year, once a week, is that they have to write a blog post about something they found on that feed." Clarence assesses his students' participation in international blogs using the rubric in figure 3.1 (pages 54-55).

After setting up the feeds that the students use as their background reading, Clarence is ready to begin having his students interact with students abroad. Using a variety of organizations, websites, and Twitter, Clarence identifies potential teacher collaborators. He generally makes contact via email at first and follows up with a Skype call to make sure the collaboration is a good fit. Of course, the fit has to make sense from a curriculum standpoint—are the two classrooms studying similar topics in similar ways? Are the two teachers in sync regarding assignments, timelines, and assessments?

Once the collaboration has been agreed to, Clarence and his partner teacher have the students get to know each other by having them fill out a survey, finding someone who is similar in the partner classroom, and leaving comments on that person's blog. Clarence pointed out that whether he collaborates with one classroom or two, the teacher partners attempt to think of the classroom as one big classroom full of kids, albeit thousands of miles apart.

After the students get to know each other, they get down to more academic work together. Clarence's project during the 2010–2011 school year focused on *The Book Thief* (Zusak, 2007). When Clarence is collaborating with a class in a time zone that allows, he reads aloud part of the featured book to both classrooms over Skype. He also has the students use a chat room in TodaysMeet (http://todaysmeet .com) during the read-aloud to talk about what is being read. "It is amazing the questions kids have during the read-aloud," Clarence said. "There's so much going on in their heads."

	1 Beginner	2 Capable	3 Accomplished	4 Expert
Commenting	• Never comments on own or others' work • Few comments approved in own space	• Rarely comments on own or others' work • Comments in own space approved late	• Regularly comments on own and others' work • Comments are approved in a timely manner	• Often comments on the work of others • Comments in own space to build community • Comments ask questions and drive forward-thinking
Developing a Global Understanding	• Accesses information only from North America • No understanding of global events and issues • Never creates own content about global issues	• Accesses information from at least two continents regularly • Little understanding of global events and issues • Rarely creates own content about global issues	• Accesses information from at least three continents regularly • Some understanding of global events and issues • Sometimes creates own content about global issues	• Accesses information from at least three continents regularly • Shows clear understanding of current global events and issues • Regularly creates own content about global issues
Connecting and Networking	• Displays rude behavior online • Gives out personal information online • Only has teacher-provided RSS feeds • No thought given to creating or sustaining a network	• Usually uses proper netiquette • Usually connects with others safely • Regularly reviews self-chosen RSS feeds • Network changes only with support	• Uses proper netiquette • Connects with others safely • Regularly reviews self-chosen RSS feeds • Network sometimes changes, growing or shrinking slowly	• Supportive of others online • Connects with others safely • Regularly reviews RSS feeds subscribed to • Deletes and adds feeds as needed • Network is flexible, changing to meet needs

Checklist

Do you . . .

- ☐ Regularly read and approve comments in your own space?
- ☐ Regularly read and comment on the work of others?
- ☐ Know what kinds of things have been written lately by people in your online community?
- ☐ Read blogs when needed?
- ☐ Listen to podcasts when needed?
- ☐ Watch videos when needed?
- ☐ Regularly review your RSS feeds, deciding which are useful and which are not?
- ☐ Regularly look for new sources of information when you have something new to learn?
- ☐ Talk to people from several continents?
- ☐ Produce information of your own in more than one form?
- ☐ Write comments that ask questions?
- ☐ Know how to use a service to translate websites in other languages?
- ☐ Have news sources from other countries in your RSS reader?
- ☐ Create content about issues that are taking part in other countries?
- ☐ Create content about ideas that you learned about from reading/watching the work of others?

Figure 3.1: Clarence Fisher's rubric for international blog participation.

Commenting on criticism that kids aren't really focusing on the book if they're chatting during the read-aloud, Clarence responded, "When you're doing a read-aloud, you often let kids doodle or draw, and that helps them concentrate, so how is it any different? I think it's actually a great value added. It's turned into a huge set of formative assessments for us. We have a wall with sticky notes [available], and we leave a question we want them to react to. So at the end of the day, we have reactions." The students place the sticky notes at a site called lino (http://en.linoit.com).

For a culmination to *The Book Thief* project, the students designed a field guide to the town where the book took place. This field guide grew into a larger project as the students also amassed details, in a Google Doc, about the various historical characters that appear in the book. Clarence required four students per each writing group, some from each classroom. "They used the chat rooms in Google

Docs," Clarence remembered. "They organized themselves into a group. Two kids wrote while the other two kids found information for them." This project turned into a hard copy book that the class published using Lulu (www.lulu.com). Clarence was able to set up a Skype interview with the author of *The Book Thief*, Markus Zusak, and ended up sending a copy of this book to Zusak. The author later told Clarence that he gave a copy of this book to his father on Father's Day.

This project was similar to one Clarence did several years ago in which his classroom collaborated with another classroom to research characteristics of the cities in which each classroom was set, called the Cities Project. For this project, Clarence's students in Snow Lake, Manitoba, collaborated with students in Haaksbergen, the Netherlands. The project involved the students' comparing and contrasting various elements of their cities. The students were given questions related to different aspects of their communities such as agriculture and electricity and were expected to answer them.

Cities Project
By Clarence Fisher

Agriculture Questions

1. What kinds of farming are found there?
2. What part of the working population is concerned with farming?
3. What is the average size of farms:
   a. arable farming
   b. stock breeding
4. What is being grown or cultivated?
5. How much milk is being produced?
6. How much meat is being produced?
7. What are the perspectives for the future, and how are they being anticipated?

Electricity Questions

1. What is the annual usage of electricity by households and companies in Snow Lake and Haaksbergen?
2. Where are the power stations that supply Snow Lake and Haaksbergen located?
3. What are the different ways that electricity is generated in Snow Lake and Haaksbergen?
4. Are environmentally safe ways of generating electricity being considered? If yes, why and in what way?

5. What are the perspectives for the future; how are they being anticipated?

Industry Questions

1. What kind of industrial companies can be found?

2. Where are industrial zones or sites located?

3. What factors make these locations especially suitable for industry?

4. What part of the working population is employed in industry?

5. What are the perspectives for the future; how are they being anticipated?

Overall Questions

1. What is the annual water consumption in Snow Lake and Haaksbergen: by households and by companies?

2. What measures have been taken to control wastewater flows?

3. Where are the points of assembly?

4. What happens there: what kinds of processing take place?

5. What are the perspectives for the future; how are they being anticipated?

Recently, Clarence has used WordPress (http://wordpress.org) to create Idea Hive (Fisher, 2009). "It's a WordPress MultiUser [or WordPress MU] setup," Clarence explained. "You can have a bunch of blogs in WordPress MultiUser. It's also got BuddyPress installed over it, which is software that will allow you to have discussion groups. It's basically an entire community."

According to Clarence, Drupal (http://drupal.org) is also used by many teachers, as is Facebook (www.facebook.com) for classroom collaborations. Twitter (http://twitter.com) is also a valuable, completely free resource for teachers who are interested in beginning international collaborations. Many Twitter accounts have an international focus. Here are a few to get you started:

- @GlobalPost
- @UN
- @LATimesworld
- @Reuters_TopNews
- @SPIEGEL_English
- @MiaFarrow
- @davos (World Economic Forum)
- @HumanRightsgov
- @NATOSource

- @MSF_USA (Doctors Without Borders)
- @UN_Women
- @UNrightswire
- @nytimesglobal
- @WFP (World Food Programme)
- @amnesty
- @UNICEF

Looking at International Collaborations From the Other Side of the World

I had a chance to speak with one of Clarence's teacher partners, Kim Cofino, who teaches at Yokohama International School (YIS) in Japan. The students in her school are children of parents who work for multinational corporations. The school uses the primary, middle years, and high school International Baccalaureate curriculum.

According to Kim, "by connecting, collaborating, and creating with other students around the world on a regular basis, students are learning how to communicate across physical, cultural, and socioeconomic boundaries. The technology we use at YIS allows students to connect with an authentic global audience on a regular basis, giving them the opportunity to build their understanding of an interconnected global society."

Kim pointed to *Third Culture Kids* (Pollock & Van Reken, 2009) as well as Mary Hayden's books on international education as major influences on her thinking. Kim has spent a good portion of her career working with these *third culture kids*. A third culture kid is defined as being a "person who has spent a significant part of his or her developmental years outside the parents' culture. The third culture kid frequently builds relationships to all of the cultures, while not having full ownership in any" (Pollock & Van Reken, 2009, p. 13).

Much of Kim's work centers on student blogs as vehicles for learning and connecting with other blogging students from across the world. In 2012, her class connected with another international school in Myanmar (http://isychinthe6 .edublogs.org) and one in Switzerland (http://blogs.zis.ch/llc/student-bloggers). In the following blog post (originally posted September 5, 2010), Kim explained how she provided her sixth-grade students with a four-step project that gave them an in-depth overview of blogs.

Part 1: Investigate

I provide the students with a list of blogs [Cofino, 2010a] to start with, and after they review at least two from my selection they can review as many of their own favorite blogs as they want (with prior approval from me). Just for fun, we reviewed one of my favorite ramen blogs in class first. We were all salivating by the end of class, and the students really understood that they can blog about anything they are passionate about, even if it's as simple as a bowl of noodles.

In order to bring in another useful skill, we're completing the reviews on Google Docs so I was able to introduce the students to their GApps accounts and the concept of collaborative note taking. In this case, each student is filling out their own review form (and sharing with me), but I'm sure we'll circle back to collaborating on a single GDoc soon enough. I was really impressed with how quickly they picked up the idea of creating a duplicate copy of the Blog Research sheet [Cofino, 2010c] (and so thankful that we used GDocs since within the first half hour two students had accidentally closed their browser window, which would have resulted in lost work had we been using Office).

Our next step is to start brainstorming a potential blogging focus by exploring our own interests. We'll most likely be using Inspiration to create a well-organized mind map of ideas that each student can blog about (in addition to their academic posts). I'm hoping that if we concentrate a bit on their personal interests, their blog will become more than just a school project. A few of the girls have already come up to me super excited about their own blogging ideas. I would love to see their unique voices start to shine through in their posts instead of always reading the same post from every student (which can so often happen when blogging becomes "homework").

Once they have some ideas about what they might be able to blog about, as well as the features of a quality blog, we'll spend some time exploring WordPress.

The final part of the Investigate stage will be reflecting on what we've learned so far and what needs to come next.

Part 2: Plan

Once that part of the project is complete, we'll begin the planning. I like to use Konrad Glogowski's How to Grow a Blog process [Glogowski, 2007]. I've used it peripherally before with middle school students.

We'll do a little bit of design work, potentially exploring a little Photoshop, so students have a chance to design custom headers at least (since the themes are all pretty much set) and probably determine which widgets they will use based on the look of their theme and header. I usually like to have them plan out what a finished product will look like in colored pencils so they focus on the design work before

Continued→

they actually get to the computer. That way their time spent actually creating their finished work is really productive.

I may also have them design a simple sitemap to really understand the purpose of (and difference between) categories, tags, archives, calendars, etc. This always seems to be a difficult piece to work in when I'm coaching in the classroom; there's just never enough time to really explore tagging and categories, so students always end up with dozens of posts [that are] uncategorized. Teachers struggle to understand the potential of a blog as eportfolio without that kind of structure.

Finally, we'll reflect before we move on to the next stage.

Part 3: Create

Only after they bring in their signed permission slips, will we actually create the blogs. This will be the shortest part of the project because they will have done the majority of the thinking, planning, and designing already. I'd love to have them publish a few pieces of work from different classes using pictures, videos, VoiceThreads, or other embeddable objects during this time. Most likely we'll also talk about the power of linking and start writing posts which connect to other students' posts in class (or around school).

Hopefully at this stage, we will also be able to connect with other blogging partners around the world. And, of course, we'll do a little bit of reflecting before moving on to the final stage.

Part 4: Evaluate

This final part of the project will focus on evaluating the success of the blogs we created, as well as the process of creating them. It would be nice to be able to have some external evaluation of our blogs in addition to individual reflection, so maybe we'll come up with a Google Form for feedback as well.

Kim's students' blogs are eventually turned into eportfolios based on goals set during student-led parent conferences. The directions in the following exercise take students through the process of transforming their nascent blogs into showcase portfolios that become a central part of teacher-student-parent conferences.

Creating a Showcase Portfolio
By Kim Cofino

In order to help you be more prepared to discuss your learning with your parents, we will create a Showcase Portfolio page on our blogs. You can include this page on your navigation menu at the top of your blog.

What to Include

- Your Student-Led Conference (SLC) goals (that we worked on a few weeks ago)
- A brief reflection on each goal: Did you meet your goal? Why or why not? Did it help you this year?
- Special pieces of work that you would like to highlight
- A visual or a link for each piece of work you are highlighting—even if you don't have a link or a visual for a piece, you should still include the piece of work. You can take a picture of it anytime before school ends and then include it in your portfolio later.
- A brief description of why this piece of work is special

Types of Work That You Might Like to Include

- Things you're proud of
- Things you did well on
- Things you found interesting
- Things you thought were fun
- Things you learned a lot from

Steps to Complete Your Showcase Portfolio

1. Create a new page on your blog.
2. Call your page Showcase or Showcase Portfolio or Portfolio.
3. Add a title: Grade 6 (next year we'll add a new section for grade 7, and so on).
4. Type your goals from your SLC document.
5. Type your reflections for each goal.
6. Determine which pieces of work you want to highlight—these may be the same pieces from SLC (but it's OK if they're not).
7. Find examples for each piece of work you're highlighting—could be a blog link, a picture, or a video—add them to your page.
8. Type a description for each piece, ask yourself:
   - Why did you include this piece?
   - What did you learn from this piece/experience?
   - What are your next steps with this piece of work/experience?
9. Add your Showcase Portfolio page to your navigation menu at the top of your blog (in Appearance > Menus).

Kim summarizes her philosophy regarding 21st century literacy in her own blog:

The goal of 21st century literacy is to move beyond obsessing about the terminology and the technology, to accept that technology is a crucial and critical aspect of our lives, and that as such, it must be used as a tool to better understand our world, to search for solutions to the problems facing our global society, and to develop a better and brighter future. 21st century literate students and teachers are those who understand that their learning and creativity can, and should, directly and positively impact our world.

All and all, my big three concepts for 21st century literacy are that students and teachers must be:

Effective Learners

Students and teachers will understand that learning is a lifelong process and that the pace of technological change requires us to focus on learning *how* to learn, rather than learning specific tools. It is expected that neither students nor teachers will know how to use every available tool, rather that they will be comfortable learning how to use new tools independently.

Independent learning requires that students and teachers are able to evaluate information for authenticity, relevance and bias as well as evaluate tools for applicability and effectiveness. As independent learners, teachers and students will be able to filter out unimportant stimuli and information so that they can focus on the important and useful, to be able to navigate graphical interfaces as well as different types of text and media formats.

Lifelong learners are reflective, they routinely practice metacognition to think about how and why they understand what they do, and they constantly strive to look deeper at their own thinking, processes and practices. Lifelong learners are intrinsically motivated to better understand the world around them and to use that knowledge for self-improvement.

Effective Collaborators

Students and teachers will develop the behaviors, attitudes and dispositions required for working in partnership with others, whether in person or over distances. Global collaboration requires effective communication, social and cultural awareness, and flexibility. Effective collaborators actively take responsibility for their role, and are able to delegate or share responsibility when necessary. Effective collaborators are equally comfortable as either leaders or participants. Effective collaborators appreciate and internalize the essential interdependence of all human endeavors.

Effective Creators

Students and teachers will understand that an essential component of lifelong learning is analyzing, synthesizing and applying what they've learned to make an original contribution to society. Effective creators are critical thinkers who are able to "think outside the box" and analyze systems to identify and solve problems. Effective creators are constantly innovating and routinely use metacognition skills to evaluate and improve their own work. Effective creators are goal oriented, using time management and multitasking skills in order to work at their highest level of productivity. Effective creators understand that, as members of an interdependent society, their work must adhere to standards of ethics and social responsibility. (Cofino, 2007a)

In the next chapter, I will interview Kim's headmaster as well as talk to other educators who are seeing what happens to global education when the students are actually physically traveling overseas.

4

THE CLASSROOM IN THE WORLD

Certainly one of the most direct ways of increasing global awareness in students is to take them overseas and allow them to experience international travel and study. Talking with Kim Cofino opened up the world of international schools to me, bringing to light those students who have spent perhaps their entire lives abroad. One would think they would be more inclined to be globally aware than would those students who have spent their whole lives in one country. In talking with the headmaster at Kim's school, James MacDonald, however, it quickly became apparent that kids can become out of touch with the world no matter where in the world they are. The Global Citizen Diploma that James describes is a project that is designed to get students out of their comfort zones regardless of where they live.

Global Citizen Diploma

As Kim explained, it's important to teach global education in international schools, because their students are sheltered: "In international schools, they're usually families who are well off or the business has paid for them. They live this global lifestyle that is a little more lavish than back in their home country. So kids who go to international schools can relate well to kids from other international schools, but not necessarily to other kids from the country in which they're in."

James MacDonald, headmaster of the YIS, does not want his students to be cut off from their surrounding culture. The students do not try to avoid being out in the world; they simply "haven't had a lot of interaction with different types of people, for example, those who are very poor. . . . When you're a young student, and this environment is what you know, you can fall into believing that yours is a 'normal life.' So I think it's part of our role and responsibility, especially because we can assume our students are going to have some access to some fantastic colleges and then go on to impressive careers, they have to be part of the solution to the problems that their generation is facing, and this can only happen if they can understand the world around them to a greater extent."

This is why YIS began the Global Citizen Diploma (GCD) Program, which is, according to James, "a backwards-by-design model, trying to look at the key elements we would identify in global citizens." In creating the Global Citizen Diploma, YIS asked for feedback from teachers, parents, and alumni; what were their top priorities? "One thing that somewhat surprised me was that the parents . . . saw the need for a significant focus on communication skills. If there was one thing that came out of the survey, it was how tuned in parents and alumni are in terms of valuing public speaking skills, writing, and a love of reading. If you rewind twenty years ago, I suspect we would have seen a lot more focus on math and science from parents," James said.

Entrepreneurial skills are also important, but as James pointed out, "you can't teach entrepreneurialism. You have to teach the skills around it: leadership, creativity. It's [the same with globalization]. It's not a class one signs up for. It's something that is learned by being exposed to it and understanding the implications."

A key emphasis of the diploma is to encourage service learning on a global scale. For example, after the tragic earthquake that occurred north of Yokohama on March 11, 2011, the school decided to adopt two schools in the damaged area. Kim elaborated, "YIS is supporting our two adopted sister schools in Tohoku in many different ways, from financial support through our Tohoku Relief charity, to material support like clothing, computers, and other school equipment, to moral and social support through collaborative events like our Cross Country Day when a group of Tohoku students came down to participate with us. We are building a strong bond with these two local Japanese schools in the Ishinomaki region that will last well beyond the immediate recovery needs that we are focused on at the moment."

James quotes Campbell's law as an argument against excessive reliance on standardized tests in schools: the more one uses a quantitative measure to make a decision, the more corrupt that measure becomes (Campbell, 1975). He added, "The Global Citizen Diploma is not designed to explicitly teach the students anything; rather, it is designed to recognize the many great things our kids are already accomplishing at a school like ours. Our current systems of educational qualifications focus almost exclusively on recognizing and rewarding academic achievement, yet we all know that shaping young people is not a purely classroom exercise and much learning happens outside of what we might call 'academics.' For example, every year our students have a week out of school visiting different parts of Japan and learning more about the culture, dozens of our students are engaged in charity work in Cambodia, the vast majority speak two or more languages, and we have been hosting a Global Issues Network conference for the past two years here. These activities cannot help but make students more globally aware, but at the same time, they are not reflected in an SAT score or an IB Diploma grade. We would all agree, however, that they go so far in defining who our students are as human beings. As such, we should be recognizing these accomplishments and using the diploma criteria to shape our school and demonstrate our practical interpretation of our mission statement."

The following explains the requirements of the Global Citizen Diploma Program as developed by the YIS. James and his teachers have been true to their desire to view test scores and grades as only part of what makes for a truly global citizen.

The YIS Global Citizen Diploma Program
By the Yokohama International School (2011d)

The YIS Global Citizen Diploma is a new diploma unique to our school that aims to complement the IB Diploma (YIS, 2011b; www.yis.ac.jp/page.cfm?p=763) and foster the skills and experiences that create globally aware and accomplished graduates. Starting with the requirements of the IB Diploma Program as its academic foundation, the GCD incorporates a range of other important

Continued→

criteria reflecting our mission to "inspire students and to provide them with the academic and social skills that will enable them to fulfill their human potential as responsible global citizens."

The program consists of three levels of certifications (Yokohama International School, 2011a; www.yis.ac.jp/page.cfm?p=1833), Global Citizen Certificate, Global Citizen Diploma, and Global Citizen Diploma with Distinction, which are explained in detail on this site. GCD program activities and achievements will be incorporated into the student's digital portfolio, which is an online space that the student, teachers, and parents can use to monitor the student's progress. Students will be mentored on meeting the Global Citizen Diploma requirements throughout their high school years by their tutors and other appointed staff supervisors.

To achieve a *Global Citizen Certificate*, a student must complete:

- All three Core Elements
- At least one of the Extended Elements

To achieve a *Global Citizen Diploma*, a student must complete:

- All three Core Elements
- The Extended Academics Element
- At least five additional Extended Elements

To achieve a *Global Citizen Diploma with Distinction*, a student must complete:

- All three Core Elements
- All eight Extended Elements
- All three Advanced Elements

Extended Elements

The eight Extended Elements offer the opportunity for students who have completed the Core Elements to receive additional certificates of achievement. To achieve the Global Citizen Diploma, students must complete all three Core Elements, the Extended Academics Element, and five additional Extended Elements.

1. **Academics**

   Requirements: Students must complete the IBDP with a grade point average of 3.4 or higher.

   Achievement: Students' grade point averages are calculated based on class performance over their high school career. Those students who narrowly miss the requirement can appeal, and in some cases other academic factors (such as predicted IB grades) will be taken into consideration.

   Evaluation: Grade point averages are indicated on report cards and transcripts.

2. **Personal Goal**

   Requirements: Students must set a personal goal outside of their comfort zone or for something that would be a stretch to accomplish. The process has three stages: (1) set the goal, (2) work towards achieving the goal, and (3) reflect on the process.

Achievement: The goal could be something involving a school activity, such as running for office, auditioning for a play, trying out for a sports team, or improving one's grades; or the goal could be a challenge independent of school life, such as running a marathon or climbing Mt. Fuji.

Evaluation: Tutors will approve the goals and ensure that they are reasonable and safe. Students will reflect on their experience and outcomes in their digital portfolio.

3. **Management**

Requirements: Students must demonstrate management of a project, activity, or significant event, with evidence of a sustained commitment.

Achievement: Students can fulfill the management requirement through school activities or outside of school. Some examples of qualifying roles include organizing a major student event, managing a fundraising activity, managing a sports team, managing a project for a local church, or managing a business activity.

Evaluation: Tutors will approve the management project. Students will reflect on their experience in their digital portfolio and upload evidence of their performance.

4. **Apprenticeship**

Requirements: Students must undertake a meaningful internship or work experience at an approved organization or learn significant skills relating to a trade, for a minimum of 100 hours. The experience can be paid or unpaid.

Achievement: Some examples of qualifying work experiences include starting and managing a business, completing a summer or part-time job, or learning trade skills.

Evaluation: Tutors will approve qualifying work experience. Students will reflect on and upload evidence from their work experience in their digital portfolio.

5. **Fit for Life**

Requirements: Students must demonstrate a commitment to healthy living through diet and lifestyle choices. Healthy living includes attention to one's mental and physical well-being.

Achievement: Students must complete four elements: (1) create a project to promote a healthy school community, (2) write a blog demonstrating their commitment to be fit for life, (3) complete a health course included in the school curriculum, and (4) complete a first aid certification (provided by the school nurse).

Evaluation: Students will reflect on their projects in their digital portfolios. The health course and first aid certification will be completed and evaluated within the school.

6. **Arts for Life**

Requirements: Students must make a significant contribution to the school's arts program or demonstrate significant creative skills outside of school.

Achievement: Students may participate in school arts activities, such as a drama production, Tanner Ensemble, Japanese music ensemble, band, or the visual arts, or they may be involved in artistic activities outside of school.

Continued→

Evaluation: Tutors and Arts Department teachers will approve students' participation. Students will reflect on their experience in their digital portfolio and upload evidence of their activity.

7. **Adventure**

Requirements: Students must show significant participation in an experiential or outdoor program that will contribute to their personal and social development through teamwork, exposure to a new environment, and a sense of personal achievement.

Achievement: Students may fulfill the requirement through developing specific skills such as hill-walking, sailing, canoeing, mountain biking, environmental protection programs, and so on. There may also be opportunities to fulfill the Adventure Element on Field Studies excursions.

Evaluation: Students will reflect on their experience in their digital portfolio and upload evidence of their activity.

8. **Digital Citizenship**

Requirements: Students must create a digital portfolio, create a tutorial video to promote digital communication, and demonstrate proper and responsible use of digital technology over the course of their high school career.

Achievement: Students must complete three requirements: (1) create a digital portfolio that shows their progress in meeting the requirements of the Global Citizen Diploma, (2) collaborate with other students to create an online tutorial video to teach one facet of what it means to be a digital citizen, which will be shown to peers and kept at YIS as a resource, and (3) follow school policies on responsible use of technology.

Evaluation: Tutors will oversee the digital portfolio and video production. Peers will provide feedback on videos. Through the YIS curriculum, students will be educated on what is appropriate to put on public blogs and the proper use of YIS technology resources.

Advanced Academics

Requirements: Students must complete the IBDP with a grade point average of 3.8 or higher and be functionally bilingual.

Achievement: Students' grade point averages are calculated based on class performance over their high school career. Language ability is assessed in language courses and exams.

Evaluation: Grade point averages are indicated on report cards and transcripts.

Advanced Personal Accomplishment

Requirements: Students must complete a substantial personal project or achieve an extraordinary personal accomplishment exceeding the Personal Goal Extended Element.

Achievement: The accomplishment must be substantial and will most likely take place outside of school. Examples of qualifying accomplishments include publishing a book, winning a national competition, competing for a national sports team, or starting a successful business venture.

Evaluation: Students will reflect on their experience in their digital portfolio and present evidence of their achievement.

Leadership

Requirements: Students must take on a substantial leadership role, with sustained commitment, either within or outside of school.

Achievement: Students will take on a role that requires the essential skills of being able to keep a team together and assert authority when required. Examples of qualifying leadership positions include president of the student council, captain of a sports team, and so on.

Evaluation: Tutors will approve qualifying positions. Students will reflect on their experience in their online portfolio and present evidence of their role.

Educators who might be interested in creating their own version of a global citizen diploma program will probably be most interested in the process that James describes that led to the creation of the YIS Global Citizen Diploma Program. Parents, teachers, administrators, and students were brought together to brainstorm and eventually delineate key characteristics of what makes for a truly global citizen. These characteristics could then form the criteria for awarding the diploma. The conversation leading up to the creation and distribution of the award was extremely valued by James, his staff, and community.

Studying Abroad

There are many programs for taking students abroad, but one of the most fascinating models is the THINK Global School. I spoke with Brad Ovenell-Carter, founding head of THINK Global School, about his experiences working in a school whose slogan is "12 countries in 12 trimesters."

Those involved in the start-up did their research and looked at similar programs, such as Class Afloat (www.classafloat.com), but ultimately decided they would start from scratch. Rather quickly, the format of the school took shape, steering toward the IB diploma program as its ultimate goal. The plan was for students to spend each part of the year in a different location. During the 2010–2011 school year, for example, the students and staff spent one term in Stockholm, one in Sydney, and one in Beijing. During the 2011–2012 year, they were in Cuenca, Ecuador; Chiang Mai, Thailand; and Berlin, Germany.

The school put high demands on the staff; there were only seven educators— one staff member for each of the core subjects, math, science, humanities, Mandarin, Spanish, fine arts, and world literature. The overarching essential question in designing the school was, What does a pure global curriculum look like?

Their goal, according to Brad, was "to turn out leaders in whatever community they wanted to return to."

In addition to the school's curriculum, the staff also had to think about the logistics. They would partner with a host school in whatever location they were in, giving the teachers and students access to such things as science labs. They had an advance team who went into the location ahead of time. Brad said, "They would recruit a local expert [who] . . . would find a residence for us, sort out transportation for us." For example, in Stockholm, the advance person would obtain subway passes; in Beijing, the advance person would secure a bus. "The teachers would give [them] a list of speakers, museums, and the advance team would start [arranging] bookings."

But no matter how thorough the preparation, there could be no school without students, and part of the challenge of this start-up school was to find students who would thrive in such a learning environment. "We scoured the world for fifteen students," said Brad. "Tuition fees are $125,000 per year. We didn't want only kids who could afford that. We had a huge scholarship fund set up." The goal was also to have a diverse blend of student backgrounds. "We had a girl in a village in Ghana who had never held an electronic device in her life . . . We were trying to get representation from all the continents. The main criteria were that we wanted solid academic students. The other key thing was that we wanted kids who had a pretty strong sense of personal identity." They also wanted students who could communicate well with adults, because the school would be featuring experts with whom the students would have to interact. Applications were collected until the end of January 2010. The initial staff were hired in April 2010, and the school began in the fall of 2010.

Once admitted to the school, students were given access to technology. For one reason, Facebook became a key orientation vehicle, in that the incoming students were encouraged to get to know each other on Facebook so that they would come in already knowing a lot about each other: "Our first day, it was more like homecoming in Stockholm," remembered Brad. "They all knew each other, because they had been on Facebook since February. There's tremendous value in social media, because kids connect." The students soon connected even more as they worked together very closely over the intense school year.

The teachers found that it was important to have students with different perspectives learning together on the road. Brad gave an example of how valuable the different perspectives were when, during the first term, the students read *Popular Music from Vittula* by Mikael Niemi (2003). "He plays with time in the book," Brad said. "A chapter might cover fifteen minutes, and a shorter chapter might cover five months." Brad asked the class why this would be, but he soon realized he was looking at the book from his own Western literary perspective. "I got these blank looks from [our] Asian kids from Thailand and Bhutan. To the Asian kids, it was, 'Well, of course time is elastic. Why would we even question it?' The whole book had now changed."

As Brad was the literature teacher, he wanted very much to include local literature from wherever they currently were. He worked with a curriculum developer who drew titles from the IB world literature booklist. He also contacted teachers in the sites where they were going to be staying. Before going to Beijing, for example, Brad discovered that the novel is not a dominant art form as it is in the West. So, he focused on Chinese poetry and also the "Monkey stories," famous for centuries in Chinese culture. In the end, the students read some 8th century Chinese poetry set against the Great Wall as they toured the Wall itself with leading Great Wall expert William Lindsay.

"We would have a mix of classes and experiential things," recalled Brad. "We might start the day with a class in our hostel, jump on a subway to the host school to have a class there, particularly if we needed a lab. Then we might leave and go to a museum for the afternoon." For physical education, the students learned fencing in Sweden, rock climbing in Australia, and tai chi in China. They studied marine biology in Sydney and then went scuba diving. These kinds of experiential learning were the main motif of this globalized school. As the students had all of these experiences, they would be required to record them in some fashion, and tagging became key. Tagging is a kind of an informal classification system in which people attach names or "tags" to online texts. If a person is writing online about a certain book, for example, the online text could be tagged by attaching the name of the book, the author, and any topic areas that are present in the book. Websites that host blogs usually allow bloggers to insert tags that are attached to any post. "We used a tagging system instead of filing," said Brad. "Students got in that habit of tagging everything. . . . As a lit teacher, when you're doing your Google SketchUp, [you] can see the math work alongside" due to the tagging system. (Google SketchUp is an online drafting tool.)

Brad spoke of the informal experiences they had together as some of the most memorable. Living so closely with each other broke down the rigid barriers between "in school" and "out of school." According to Brad, "The interdisciplinary work happened all the time. When we were going somewhere—on a bus or train to the Blue Mountains outside Sydney, for example—a kid would approach the math teacher, and everyone in the bus would hear that discussion . . . The value was that we were all living with each other all the time . . . A lot of our conversations would occur at the dinner table. It was just-in-time learning."

Brad was impressed with how much work they could do in a year in such an informal setting: "It was very clear to me that by our third term, school was a habit of mind, not a place. We could be anywhere as a group, and I would say, 'OK, let's have a class' and there would be total focus."

Brad believes that the school has met the goal of helping to form global citizens: "A global citizen would be able to pick up a major newspaper and understand it cover to cover. They would read a sports [page] and have seen [and understood] cricket and hockey. They would see in entertainment pop culture symbols used around the world, but they would also recognize gamelan or traditional Chinese music. When they look at a home section, they would understand why homes are laid out this way as opposed to in Berlin . . . I feel like in a year I got up high enough to see where [education] is going. I think everyone is going to go down these paths. I think they are going to look at these things, and the successful ones are going to move toward open and trusting schools."

Brad's experiences are certainly difficult, if not impossible, for most teachers to emulate. For most teachers today, field trips are out of reach from an organizational and financial standpoint. However, the THINK Global School can provide a template for setting up virtual field trips that are multidisciplinary in nature. In fact, it would be an interesting assignment to tell students about the THINK Global School and assign them to curate their own collection of texts to study that could be associated with various locations across the world. Of course, there is no substitute for international travel in broadening global awareness. However, in the absence of the ability to travel, the THINK Global School format can provide motivation for armchair wanderers.

Homeschools and Alternative Schools

"Warning: Unsocialized homeschoolers." This statement was on a bumper sticker I saw pasted on the back of a vehicle parked at the local library. The creators of the bumper sticker were obviously playing with the commonly held belief that homeschoolers are doomed to a life of loneliness, having gone through childhood in relative isolation. But does this joke still work in a web 2.0 world when it's easy to be connected with hundreds if not thousands of "friends" both close to home and on an international level? What are the implications for curriculum and instruction when so many students are learning outside the proverbial four walls? The homeschooling population continues to grow, somewhat under the radar, increasing from approximately 15,000 homeschool students in the 1960s in the United States to between 1.5 and 2 million in 2010 (National Home Education Research Institute, 2010).

I first began interviewing homeschooling families a few years ago, as I discovered that many of them were taking advantage of the freedom they have to use technology and structure assignments that include new literacies. I have found that many homeschooling families include activities that involve their children reaching out to the entire world. These are schools in which there truly are no structural barriers to being globalized. For these educators, time is not an issue, a curriculum "core" is a matter of choice, and any website blocking is a matter solely of personal choice. How are homeschoolers taking advantage of new media in the education of their students?

As evidenced by the bumper sticker, a commonly held stereotype of homeschoolers is that they are sitting alone filling out worksheets. The irony of this is that many homeschooled students are actually more engaged with the world than traditionally schooled students. Indeed, what comes across frequently when talking with homeschooled students is how they are actually doing things—as volunteers, as entrepreneurs, as activists—instead of sitting passively listening to a teacher talk about people who do things.

It is clear that in homeschools (just as in traditional schools) the advent of technology has transformed the learning activities that are possible, and there are homeschooling families who are taking advantage of these opportunities. For example, one of the homeschooling parents I interviewed, Martha (her name has been changed), spoke the most animatedly about technology when she talked about how her sons are in a band and how her husband has helped them create a site on MySpace, an additional website, and a video posted on YouTube to publicize their music on a national and international level. "The band is part of their schooling," she said. This follows with her feeling that all of life can count as part of her children's education. "If you're living and breathing, you're learning," she said. Regarding the band, in addition to becoming better musicians, "they're learning how to manage their money. They've sold CDs. They're learning how to run a little business."

A former homeschooled student, Rachel, now in her twenties, also remembers the relative freedom she experienced as a homeschooled student, allowing her to experience activities, even international travel, that a traditionally schooled student would not have been able to experience. Rachel's first memory of being homeschooled, in fact, revolves around her realization of this key freedom difference: "My first memory of being homeschooled, was a day I was outside catching bugs. We caught a praying mantis. My mom made a little science lesson out of this experience. This would have never happened in a traditional school. There was a lot more freedom to it."

Rachel's mother began to homeschool her when she was in fourth grade, and almost immediately, Rachel began volunteering at a local food bank, a daycare center, and a local historic site. By the age of ten, she was volunteering as a docent at the site, giving tours to schoolchildren on field trips who were older than she was. Rachel remembers the time she was almost put on the bus to return to a school, because the teacher assumed she was one of the schoolchildren.

The homeschooling organization that Rachel's family belonged to had an international education emphasis. Each month, the homeschool students would do an extensive study on some country. The geography, culture, and history of the country would be researched by each student, and the culminating activity was to present the research to the other homeschooling families when they had their monthly assembly at a local community center. Students would dress in costume and prepare food from their assigned countries.

The confidence that Rachel gained by working as a docent and volunteer led to her first international travel experience as she was invited to apply to the People to People program and go to New Zealand and Australia when she was fifteen. She was accepted into the program and had only a few months to raise $5,000 to pay for the trip. Rachel described how she painstakingly collected aluminum cans and negotiated a good price for them at her local recycling center. She also sold notecards that she designed and eggs from the family chickens. Before she knew it, she was headed off on a very long plane ride.

She described how each of the People to People trips has a cultural or scientific focus. The topic for her trip was the animal kingdom. "We went to a lot of wild-life parks and zoos to see the strange animals," Rachel said. "I got to stay with an Australian family, and we got to stay in a Māori marae. It's a temple made out of bright red wood." She described how a feature of the marae is that it contains drawings on the wall that feature the entire history of its people and that these drawings help the community preserve its oral history. "Being able to see that as a fifteen-year-old blew my mind," she said.

But homeschoolers also have the freedom to experience various international cultural events even without physically traveling overseas. Whether it's going to a museum that has an exhibition of some ancient art from a particular culture or going to see a foreign film at the local university, homeschooled children have the chance to sample these tastes of international culture that are in their backyards. While the logistics of taking traditionally schooled students on field trips to a local museum or arts event becomes more and more difficult, the homeschooled student simply jumps in the car with the parent/teacher and goes.

Homeschooled students have the opportunity to participate in a number of community events. For example, an increasing number of communities have venues, sometimes even full-blown festivals, devoted to the exhibition of foreign films. Simply taking a student to a foreign film can broaden the student's cultural horizons. The Cleveland International Film Festival, for example, exhibits foreign films each year as part of its ten-day event. They also include a daily FilmSlam that is designed specifically for students (www.clevelandfilm.org/festival /special-programs/filmslam). Each weekday of the event, a feature film and at least one short from the festival are shown to local high school students who are bused in for the morning. These films often have an international focus and, often, either the writer, director, or one or more of the actors are present to answer questions after the film is shown. In advance of the FilmSlam, participating teachers receive Teachers' Guides with resources, including links, to the films being shown.

I talked to Beth Steele Radisek, special projects manager, about the global education implications for this project: "FilmSlam exposes junior high/high school students to a medium they love, have grown up with, and understand. The program introduces them to international cultures, lives, stories, and experiences through films they would never see in the mainstream market. By meeting the filmmakers at FilmSlam, students get immediate answers to questions about film/filmmaking. While surrounded by their peers, they can experience the magic of film." While the FilmSlam is designed for traditionally schooled children, a number of homeschooled children attend every year and can attend for more than one day, if they wish.

The opportunities for global education seem endless for homeschoolers. No matter what the subject being studied, there is a nearby museum, exhibition, or cultural event that can apply. In addition, there are many constraints that traditional teachers have that don't apply to homeschoolers.

Advantages of Homeschooling

- Ability to deal with time-zone challenges: This is frequently mentioned by traditional school teachers as a barrier for international education. Yet, for a homeschooler, Skyping or synchronously chatting is more possible, even if the North American student is having to set up the Skype or chat at odd hours of the day.

- Ability to Skype and Google Chat: Many traditional classrooms may not be equipped to conduct Skype calls or other synchronous chatting due to equipment issues. But any homeschooler with reliable broadband Internet and a laptop is equipped for international dialogue.

- Ability to go to local museums and other arts events that have an international focus: It is increasingly difficult for teachers in traditional schools to set up field trips, and if a field trip does occur, it may only happen once a year or once a semester. For homeschooling families, going to local cultural events can be weekly, even daily, events.

- Ability to travel: Physically traveling abroad is not necessary for international education but, if possible, certainly makes for an irreplaceable experience. Such travel is much easier for homeschool students.

Although the differences between homeschooling and traditional schooling may seem great, it can be argued that the lines between homeschooling and traditional schooling are blurring due to the rapid growth in online learning. An increasing number of states are requiring all high school students to take at least one online course before graduation. The popularity of online college courses is part of what is driving this movement at the high school level. Some high schools are even moving to hybrid models in which students attend a class in person several days a week and log in from home for the other days (Kist, 2010). As teachers move toward developing instruction for online classes at the high school level (and perhaps even at younger grades), homeschooling families may be looked at for inspiration. What can be done when learning activities can be structured in such a way that they can be accomplished twenty-four hours a day, seven days a week? What are the implications for increased global education when students are not confined in schools that only operate from 8:00 a.m. to 3:00 p.m. with all the connection blockage issues that often are a part of traditional education? Homeschooling educators have been taking advantage of these kinds of freedoms for years.

In the next chapter, I will summarize some of the trends I've observed in talking with the inspiring educators featured in this book.

CHAPTER 5

GETTING STARTED

There's no place like home.

Dorothy Gale

In a *New York Times* article, Michael Kimmelman (2011) asserts, "We tend to underestimate the power of physical places." The piece focuses on the "power of place," highlighting the "political power of places" such as Kent State, the Berlin Wall, Tiananmen Square, and, more recently, Tahrir Square and Zuccotti Park.

But here I am writing a book that suggests that, in the field of education at least, we may have overestimated the power of physical places. In a very real way, the four classroom walls have tended to trap teachers and students into perpetuating longstanding literacy practices and events that may reach the level of ritual (McLaren, 1986). And now, more than ever, those four walls may very easily be transcended in ways that teachers certainly couldn't have envisioned even a few years ago. What if we can "do" school anywhere at any time?

Of course, this lack of face-to-face communication is scary and depressing to many people when they think about social media in general. But I have to say, after having interviewed so many forward-thinking educators for this book, I have come away optimistic and hopeful about what the virtual spaces of the new media will bring about in our schools, and this is in no small part due to the international scope that our classrooms have. Those educators who want to take advantage of the amazing international potentials in their classrooms have some very clear steps they can take toward the goal of transcending place and time. In this chapter, I discuss some overall trends in the steps taken by the teachers I have interviewed. The following is a summary that may act as a planning guide for those interested in trying some of the ideas that have been presented.

Enlarge Your Personal Learning Network

Educators who are active in global education have strong personal learning networks (PLNs). In many cases, they have developed long-lasting professional and personal relationships that endure even with few (if any) face-to-face meetings. It's clear that PLNs are transforming staff development, as, via blogs, Twitter, and Nings, teachers have access to the leading theorists and practitioners in education, no matter what their areas of interest are. More importantly, however, these educators have access to one another, as they break out of the classroom silos that have often made the teaching profession isolating. These PLNs have impacted educators on the most routine classroom level, as teachers compare lesson plans, for example; the PLNs have also had an influence on the most systemic level, as teachers examine, through their own PLNs, the possibility of new ways of doing school.

When I work with teachers, I often hear statements such as "I just don't have time to be on Twitter" or "I have more important things to do than to spend time on Facebook looking at someone's vacation pictures." Of course, we all realize that surfing through various social network venues can be a time waster. But I'm worried for the number of teachers I encounter who seem to be willing to throw away the baby with the bath water. Instead of not participating in Twitter at all, why not just wisely choose the people you follow? If someone keeps tweeting things that aren't helpful to you as a teacher, simply stop following that person. I truly believe that just spending five minutes a day on Twitter will open anyone up to an unbelievable number of ideas for internationalizing our schools.

Start Collecting Ideas

Keep a document in which you deposit all the great ideas you find via your PLN. Be sure to keep all the links and contact information that go along with that idea. You may find you have questions later and, if you don't have the contact information or the link, it will take you much longer to track down that idea. Record any and all ideas that you think may have some merit.

Think About What's Important to Your Students

New forms of communication allow teachers and students to go beyond standardized test preparation and scripted curricula and move schools into using the power of students' minds and talents to actually do some things. Instead of spending the day memorizing facts and spitting them back on worksheets, students may be helping to contribute or even create a social justice project. Instead of proving that they can do an algorithm, they can use that algorithm to help someone half a world away. Through such efforts as the Flat Classroom Project and its spin-off projects such as Eracism, it's easy to see that the goals of such projects make goals such as memorizing facts for a test embarrassingly irrelevant and out of date. When you talk to educators like James MacDonald and Kim Cofino of the Yokohama International School, you get a sense that rote-level learning is out of some past parallel universe, almost in the way medical doctors now look at the past practice of using leeches to bleed people.

Teachers who feel that they don't have time to think about what's important to their students demonstrate that they haven't read the newest curriculum documents, because there seems to be quite a convergence in these documents that higher-level thinking should trump fact-level recall every time (Porter et al., 2011). It's clear that various college and career readiness standards support the use of these new tools for creating complex, collaborative projects that could, potentially, harness the power of the millions of students all over the world. Rather than having kids spend hours doing mindless homework, why not have them collaborate with a classroom in Africa to improve sustainability efforts or work with a cohort of students in Europe to create a framework for conflict management? What the technology gives educators is the ability to really break out of the curriculum boxes and map out a new topography for what a classroom can and will look like in the future. Take some time to talk with your students about issues that are pressing to them that could benefit from a global perspective.

Think About How the Topic Connects to the Curriculum

Of course, any teacher is going to need to write lesson plans, whether or not they are being collected and examined. As pointed out in chapter 1, most of the current curriculum frameworks in the United States advocate for cognitive complexity, suggesting the need for large-scale, problem-based projects that are perfectly aligned with global interaction and collaboration. One idea is to talk openly with students regarding the curriculum when doing these kinds of activities so that the connection to curriculum goals and objectives is explicit.

Choose Projects and Tools

Any teacher who has one computer with Internet access and the ability to access Wikispaces (www.wikispaces.com) can do the majority of what the teachers portrayed in this book are doing. When I was teaching in the late 1980s and early 1990s, just as personal computers were beginning to enter schools, I found technology to be extremely complicated and difficult to use in the classroom. It was not a user-friendly time. I well remember going to some training session about the Internet in which the trainer took us painstakingly through how to write HTML code. About five minutes after walking out of that session, I had already forgotten all of what I had learned. Today, it takes three easy steps to set up a wiki. It takes just a few steps to set up a Twitter account and follow the best minds in the global education world. It takes just a basic knowledge of how to surf the Internet to check in on the many blogs that are written on this topic or participate in an online conference related to this topic. And it's all free (as long as one has a computer and Internet access). Many of the projects described in this book are easily realizable for any teacher who has a desire to globalize his or her classroom. The challenge is to decide how to reach the desired goals. There are so many interesting and vibrant projects out there ready to be implemented for you and your students.

Create a Rubric

Most teachers must ultimately come up with a rather traditional grade for any project that is assigned in the classroom. This grade must be able to be averaged in with the remaining grades for an overall grading period grade. The answer for converting complicated projects into a gradebook grade is to develop a robust rubric for each project that is done. Most teachers have experience using rubrics, and it's clear that a rubric can be designed for anything that is being assessed. There is a well-known site, RubiStar (http://rubistar.4teachers.org), that will walk teachers through the creation of a rubric for any task, process, or artifact. But it is also a great idea to co-construct a rubric for your international project with your students. What are the main curriculum objectives that you want to assess? How will you make sure that the students have achieved those objectives?

One of the most powerful orienting activities before embarking on a project is to have a discussion with your students about the content of the rubric. Constructing the rubric with students can be a powerful way not only to come to agreement with the students as to what the goals of the project are, but also to create a community of learners with students as they see themselves as co-builders of the learning tasks. One of the challenging aspects of grading the kinds of projects that are described in this book is that they are often open-ended and ongoing. Therefore, some time lines may need to be set as part of the grading process. In other words, students need to be told that they need to be at a certain point in the project by a certain date to get the best grade (even if the project is never really finished).

Be Willing to Go Beyond Your Job Description

In many cases, the teachers profiled in this book are working on these global projects outside of the scope of their day jobs. "This is a labor of love," said Lucy Gray of the Global Education Conference. The Flat Classroom Project, also, grew out of a purely informal collaboration between two teachers from across the world for whom this project was not part of their official duties.

Be Passionate, Yet Realistic, About Global Education

The educators I interviewed for this book are passionate about global education. It is clear that they have been hooked and stay up late hours to communicate across many time zones, to finish the projects they want to get done. However, the teachers I interviewed are struggling with the barriers that we all encounter—lack of technology, lack of support, lack of time, struggles with time zones, and, of course, a continuing societal obsession with standardized curriculum and testing. But these teachers are also persevering and producing amazing results. Just as you can.

EPILOGUE

I return to Black River and see the iPads more seamlessly integrated into the kindergarten classrooms. The teachers report that the project has had some challenges. For one thing, the teachers had difficulty getting the iPads in and out of their storage carts (in which they were recharged). This problem was solved by coming up with a numbering system and marking the slots and iPads with large numbers, so it was easier to see how the iPads lined up when they were loaded.

Another problem was the syncing up of the iPads after apps were added. The technology director found that when one iPad didn't get synced correctly, then each had to be done individually, and there are eighty of them. And then they found that new apps that were added didn't get automatically put into the existing folders on the iPads. This was solved by asking some high school technology students to manually put the apps into each folder.

Cheri Hlavsa, the curriculum director, also says, "I wish we had surveyed parents as to how many of them have Internet access. At first, some parents didn't want the iPads sent home, because they don't have the Internet, but now they have received some notes from parents who now want them sent home. [Having the iPads in the home] has impacted what [families] are doing at home."

The teachers have created an organizational system on the iPads using the following folders:

- Teacher Tools
- Photography
- Two folders with books

- ABCs
- Words
- Free Choice
- Math
- Science and Social Studies

All the kindergarten teachers are impressed with how quickly the students have adopted the vocabulary of using the iPads. The students say sentences such as, "Our app is getting updated," or "You need to move your cursor." The kids are actually excited when they see the technology coordinator taking the cart away, because they know that means they will be getting new apps on their iPads. To strengthen the global emphasis of the project, the teachers have been using Google Maps and various weather apps to zoom in on spots around the world, making the daily weather something that is displayed not only on their iPads but also on the SMART Board so that it is a part of the routine discussion of the classroom. The educators believe that the global implications for their project lie in the ease of navigation of the iPad that is being displayed by very young children. As I move through the different kindergarten classrooms, I see evidence that these children are, indeed, very conversant in the interface that will probably be with them and many around the globe for years to come.

After school, I talk to a few parents who seem to be uniformly positive about the experience of having their kindergartners in possession of iPads. One parent says, "I'm shocked by how many apps he knows." Another parent whose child is autistic says that the iPad is really helpful for kids who aren't verbal at all. She says that her son really enjoys the games which are in the Free Choice folder and keeps repeating, "I'm going to make a pizza," which is related to one of the games. Parents report that their children also enjoy taking still photos and making videos with their iPads.

One parent worries about breaking the iPad. "We just leave it in the bookbag. He doesn't just throw it on his floor. . . . I almost wish they had something that covered the front screen," she says. Another concern is whether having the iPads will impact the students' handwriting abilities. One parent sees this complaint, however, as an unnecessary backlash against technology in general. She says, "They need both," meaning both the iPad and paper and pencil. "I absolutely don't want handwriting to go away. But then you want them to be able to compete on a technology level, too." Several parents note the competition between their kindergarten students and their older siblings who are jealous of their younger sibling's iPad. "If my older son is doing a worksheet, it doesn't cheer for him," says one parent.

In the end, however, the parents I talk to are extremely positive about the iPad project. "My son is a special needs student," says one parent. "I definitely see more of an interest in education on his part. He is a student I couldn't even get to write his name. With the iPad, he's doing letter recognition. The motivation is there. He has some fine motor issues, so paper and pencil are difficult for him . . . He has his favorite [apps] to do. He carries around the iPad with him and takes lots of photos. By Sunday night, he has taken 400 pictures. He also makes videos and says, 'Ready, set, action.' I enjoy that he has the opportunity to have an iPad."

Overall, my experiences visiting Black River have made me see the value in giving even very young children the ability to communicate in the very newest ways we have. This newfangled tablet has made reading and writing so attractive within these families that siblings are fighting for access. One can see that these young children will be well positioned to take part in the global conversation that will be a big part of their adult lives.

GLOSSARY

app. An abbreviation for the word *application* that has come to stand for a function that may be performed on a device such as an iPhone or iPad. People may buy an app for any number of purposes such as checking the weather, playing a game, or providing location directions, to name a few.

blog. Shortened from the term *web log*, an online journal or diary that the author can make available for readers to view and comment on.

cloud. A virtual space (other than one's hard drive) for storing files. By storing files in a virtual cloud, users can access their files from various devices connected to the Internet. Storing files in a cloud allows for greater ease of international collaboration.

digital citizenship. Being capable of taking part in discussions about world affairs that may be almost exclusively carried on in a digital environment (via social networks).

digital native. Marc Prensky (2005) suggests that people who have grown up with technology are more comfortable with using it (are "natives") as opposed to people who did not grow up with it (who Prensky calls "digital immigrants").

flat world. Concept promoted by Thomas Friedman suggesting that the new technology essentially flattens the world, so that we are all on one plane, easily able to communicate with and influence each other.

Glogster (www.glogster.com). A website that allows users to create interactive posters. The interactivity of the site allows it to function as a social network.

Google Docs. A wide-ranging service provided by Google that allows people to collaborate on documents that are housed at the Google Docs site and are able to be edited and collaborated on by those who are permitted to access the documents.

new literacies. Essentially, the many forms of representation available to us today. The "new" part of *new literacies* refers to the fact that these literacies have come about as a result of new technology and often (but not always) involve reading and writing on a screen.

Ning. A social network that has been created specifically for a certain group. Housed on Ning.com.

personal learning network (PLN). A group of colleagues who usually collaborate online and have likely never met face-to-face, who form an informal community via such platforms as Twitter, Facebook, or LinkedIn.

Prezi. Presentation software, similar to PowerPoint, used for its ability to zoom in and out of various pictures or words in a nonlinear fashion.

really simple syndication (RSS) feed. Subscription service for individual blogs and websites that automatically sends site content updates to subscribers.

smartphone. The newest generations of cell phones, first made popular by Blackberry, but now being overtaken by the iPhone, with Internet connectivity and advanced software capabilities.

tablet. The generic term for a mobile device, such as an iPad.

tagging. An informal labeling system often used by bloggers to attach certain words ("tags") to posts so that they are searchable by readers.

uniform resource locator (URL). Technical term for the address of a website. One types the URL into an Internet browser (such as Firefox) to go to a specific website.

widget. An application or a component of an interface that enables a user to perform a function or access a service, and that can often be personalized. Some examples include weather widgets like those offered through WeatherBug and the Weather Channel, which allow users to monitor and quickly access applications.

Wi-Fi. Wireless Internet connectivity.

wiki. Named after a Hawaiian word meaning "quick," a website that is collaboratively written by its users. The most famous example of a wiki is Wikipedia (www.wikipedia.org), which is an online encyclopedia written by volunteers across the world. Most classroom wikis are hosted on such free websites as Wikispaces.com or PBworks.com.

REFERENCES AND RESOURCES

American Council on the Teaching of Foreign Languages. (n.d.). *National standards for foreign language education*. Accessed at www.actfl.org/i4a/pages.index.cfm?pagesid=3392 on February 17, 2011.

Association for Library Service to Children. (2012). *Welcome to the (Mildred L.) Batchelder Award home page*. Accessed at www.ala.org/alsc/awardsgrants/bookmedia/batchelderaward on February 20, 2012.

Austin Public Library. (2009). *African American teen fiction*. Accessed at www.connectedyouth.org/books/index.cfm?booklist=afam on February 22, 2012.

Austin Public Library. (2010a). *Asian and Asian American fiction*. Accessed at www.connectedyouth.org/books/index.cfm?booklist=asian on February 22, 2012.

Austin Public Library. (2010b). *Hispanic teen fiction*. Accessed at www.connectedyouth.org/books/index.cfm?booklist=hispanicteen on February 22, 2012.

Austin Public Library. (2010c). *Middle Eastern fiction*. Accessed at www.connectedyouth.org/books/index.cfm?booklist=middle on March 13, 2012.

Beeghly, D. G. (2005). It's about time: Using electronic literature discussion groups with adult learners. *Journal of Adolescent & Adult Literacy, 49*(1), 12–21.

Borsheim, C. (2004). Email partnerships: Conversations that changed the way my students read. *English Journal, 93*(5), 60–65.

Buckingham, D. (2003). *Media education: Literacy, learning, and contemporary culture*. Cambridge, England: Polity Press.

Campbell, D. T. (1975). Assessing the impact of planned social change. In G. M. Lyons (Ed.), *Social research and public policies* (pp. 3–45). Hanover, NH: Public Affairs Center, Dartmouth College.

Charney, N. (2010). *Stealing the mystic lamb: The true story of the world's most coveted masterpiece*. New York: PublicAffairs.

Children's Literature and Reading Special Interest Group. (2011). *Notable books for a global society*. Accessed at www.clrsig.org/nbgs.php on May 10, 2012.

Cofino, Kim. (2007a, October 4). Essential understandings for 21st century literacy [Web log post]. Accessed at http://kimcofino.com/blog/2007/10/04/essential-understandings-for-21st-century-literacy on February 20, 2012.

Cofino, K. (2007b, May 15). Simulating the "real world" [Web log post]. Accessed at http://kimcofino.com/blog/2007/05/15/simulating-the-real-world on February 20, 2012.

Cofino, K. (2010a). Becoming a blogger! [Web log post]. Accessed at http://blogs.yis.ac.jp/mstech/2010/08/26/becoming-a-blogger on February 22, 2012.

Cofino, K. (2010b, September 5). Beginning with blogging [Web log post]. Accessed at http://kimcofino.com/blog/2010/09/05/beginning-with-blogging on February 20, 2012.

Cofino, K. (2010c). *Blog research*. Accessed at https://docs.google.com/document/edit?id=1OVBqVG_TfjwuunYyoNV6k0u2ZjJFM2kYTNtru1jaTwg&hl=en&authkey=COmq26wN&pli=1 on February 20, 2012.

Cofino, K. (2012). *Creating your showcase portfolio*. Accessed at http://blogs.yis.ac.jp/mstech/?s=creating+your+showcase+portfolio on May 10, 2012.

Common Core State Standards Initiative. (2011). *Common Core State Standards for English language arts & literacy in history/social studies, science, and technical subjects: The standard—English language arts standards*. Accessed at www.corestandards.org on March 2, 2012.

Cooperative Children's Book Center. (2006). *30 multicultural books every teen should know.* Accessed at www.education.wisc.edu/ccbc/books/detailListBooks.asp?idBookLists=253 on February 22, 2012.

Cooperative Children's Book Center. (2007). *Global reading: Selected literature for children and teens set in other countries.* Accessed at www.education.wisc.edu/ccbc/books/detailListBooks.asp?idBookLists=280 on February 22, 2012.

Cooperative Children's Book Center. (2011). *50 books about peace and social justice.* Accessed at www.education.wisc.edu/ccbc/books/detailListBooks.asp?idBookLists=77 on February 22, 2012.

Crosby, A. W. (1986). *Ecological imperialism: The biological expansion of Europe, 900–1900.* New York: Cambridge University Press.

Csikszentmihalyi, M. (1990). *Flow: The psychology of optimal experience.* New York: HarperCollins.

Cushner, K., & Mahon, J. (2009). Developing the intercultural competence of educators and their students: Creating the blueprints. In D. K. Deardorff (Ed.), *The SAGE handbook of intercultural competence* (pp. 304–320). Thousand Oaks, CA: SAGE.

Cuyahoga County Public Library. (2012). *Homework help.* Accessed at www.cuyahogalibrary.org/StdBackPage.aspx?id=17082 on February 22, 2012.

East, K., & Thomas, R. L. (2007). *Across cultures: A guide to multicultural literature for children.* Westport, CT: Libraries Unlimited.

Elmer, A. (2011, May 11). IdeaJam on education—with Alan November (Monday, May 2) [Web log post]. Accessed at http://engage.intel.com/thread/4548 on February 20, 2011.

Fisher, C. (2009, March 26). Idea Hive—introduction [Video file]. Accessed at www.youtube.com/watch?v=0tvCft8y2jY on February 20, 2012.

Flat Classroom. (n.d.). *Home.* Accessed at http://fcp11-3.flatclassroomproject.org/home on February 20, 2012.

Freire, P. (2000). *Pedagogy of the oppressed* (30th anniversary ed.). New York: Continuum.

Friedman, T. L. (2005). *The world is flat: A brief history of the twenty-first century*. New York: Farrar, Straus & Giroux.

Glogowski, K. (2007). *How to grow a blog*. Accessed at www.teachandlearn.ca /blog/2007/10/27/how-to-grow-a-blog on June 11, 2012.

Hathaway, R. (2011). A powerful pairing: The literature circle and the wiki. *The ALAN Review, 38*(3), 14–22.

Hull, G. A., Stornaiuolo, A., & Sahni, U. (2010). Cultural citizenship and cosmopolitan practice: Global youth communicate online. *English Education, 42*(4), 331–367.

International Baccalaureate. (2012). *Mission and strategy*. Accessed at www.ibo .org/mission on February 22, 2012.

International Board on Books for Young People. (n.d.). *Bookbird*. Accessed at www.ibby.org/index.php?id=276 on February 20, 2012.

International Children's Digital Library. (n.d.). *Index*. Accessed at http:// en.childrenslibrary.org on February 20, 2012.

Johnson, L., Smith, R., Willis, H., Levine, A., & Haywood, K. (2011). *The 2011 Horizon Report: Key trends*. Austin, TX: New Media Consortium. Accessed at http://wp.nmc.org/horizon2011/sections/trends on March 12, 2012.

Kansas Historical Society. (2012). *Traveling resource trunks*. Accessed at www .kshs.org/p/traveling-resource-trunks/14969 on February 22, 2012.

Kimmelman, M. (2011, October 15). In protest, the power of place. *The New York Times*. Accessed at www.nytimes.com/2011/10/16/sunday-review/wall-street -protest-shows-power-of-place.html?_r=1&ref=todayspaper on November 18, 2011.

Kist, W. (2000). Beginning to create the new literacy classroom: What does the new literacy look like? *Journal of Adolescent & Adult Literacy, 43*(8), 710–718.

Kist, W. (2005). *New literacies in action: Teaching and learning in multiple media*. New York: Teachers College Press.

Kist, W. (2007). Basement new literacies: Dialogue with a first-year teacher. *English Journal, 97*(1), 43–48.

Kist, W. (2010). *The socially networked classroom: Teaching in the new media age.* Thousand Oaks, CA: Corwin Press.

Klein, N. (2000). *No logo: Taking aim at the brand bullies.* New York: Picador.

Krumgold, J. (1970). *Henry 3.* New York: Washington Square Press.

Larson, L. C. (2009). Reader response meets new literacies: Empowering readers in online learning communities. *The Reading Teacher, 62*(8), 638–648.

Lehman, B. A., Freeman, E. B., & Scharer, P. L. (2010). *Reading globally, K–8: Connecting students to the world through literature.* Thousand Oaks, CA: Corwin Press.

Lindsay, J., & Davis, V. A. (2012). *Flattening classrooms, engaging minds: Move to global collaboration one step at a time.* New York: Allyn & Bacon.

Literary Link. (1998). *Historical and/or multicultural YA books.* Accessed at http://theliterarylink.com/yaauthors.html on February 22, 2012.

Lynskey, D. (2011). *33 revolutions per minute: A history of protest songs, from Billie Holiday to Green Day.* New York: Ecco.

Maltese, D., & Naughter, K. (2010). Taking down walls: An international wiki creates a community of thinkers. *Voices from the Middle, 18*(1), 17–25.

Mann, C. C. (2011). *1493: Uncovering the new world Columbus created.* New York: Knopf.

McLaren, P. (1986). *Schooling as a ritual performance: Towards a political economy of educational symbols and gestures.* London: Routledge.

McLuhan, M., & Powers, B. R. (1989). *The global village: Transformations in world life and media in the 21st century.* New York: Oxford University Press.

Meadows, D. (1990). *The Donella Meadows archive: Voice of a global citizen.* Accessed at www.sustainer.org/dhm_archive/index.php?display_article=vn338villageed on February 17, 2012.

Merriam, S. B. (1998). *Qualitative research and case study applications in education* (2nd ed.). San Francisco: Jossey-Bass.

MobiThinking. (2012). *Global mobile statistics 2012*. Accessed at http://mobithinking.com/mobile-marketing-tools/latest-mobile-stats on May 6, 2012.

Myers, J., & Eberfors, F. (2010). Globalizing English through intercultural critical literacy. *English Education, 42*(2), 148–171.

National Commission on Excellence in Education. (1983). *A nation at risk: The imperative for educational reform*. Washington, DC: U.S. Department of Education.

National Council for the Social Studies. (n.d.). *What are global and international education?* Accessed at www.socialstudies.org/positions/global/whatisglobaled on February 17, 2011.

National Council for the Social Studies. (2010). *National curriculum standards for social studies: A framework for teaching, learning, and assessment*. Silver Spring, MD: Author. Accessed at www.socialstudies.org/standards/strands on March 12, 2012.

National Governors Association Center for Best Practices, & Council of Chief State School Officers. (2010). *Common Core State Standards for English language arts & literacy in history/social studies, science, and technical subjects: Appendix B—Text exemplars and sample performance tasks*. Washington, DC: Authors. Accessed at www.corestandards.org/assets/Appendix_B.pdf on April 2, 2012.

National Home Education Research Institute. (2010). *National Home Education Research Institute*. Accessed at www.nheri.org on May 27, 2010.

National Park Service. (n.d.). *"The life of a Civil War soldier" traveling trunk: Teacher's guide*. Accessed at www.nps.gov/gett/forteachers/upload/Travel%20Trunk%20Guide.pdf on February 22, 2012.

New London Group. (1996). A pedagogy of multiliteracies: Designing social futures. *Harvard Education Review, 66*(1), 60–92.

Nielsen. (2010, June 1). The state of mobile apps [Web log post]. Accessed at http://blog.nielsen.com/nielsenwire/online_mobile/the-state-of-mobile-apps on February 20, 2012.

Niemi, M. (2003). *Popular music from Vittula*. New York: Seven Stories Press.

Paris, D. (2010). Texting identities: Lessons for classrooms from multiethnic youth space. *English Education, 42*(3), 278–292.

Partnership for 21st Century Skills. (2011a). *Environmental literacy*. Accessed at www.p21.org/overview/skills-framework/57 on March 12, 2012.

Partnership for 21st Century Skills. (2011b). *Global awareness*. Accessed at www .p21.org/overview/skills-framework/57 on February 17, 2012.

Partnership for 21st Century Skills. (2011c). *Life and career skills*. Accessed at www.p21.org/overview/skills-framework/266 on March 12, 2012.

Piaget, J. (1957). John Amos Comenius. *Prospects, 23*(1–2), 173–196.

Pink, D. H. (2005). *A whole new mind: Why right-brainers will rule the future*. New York: Penguin.

Pollock, D. C., & Van Reken, R. (2009). *Third culture kids: Growing up among worlds* (Rev. ed.). Boston: Brealey.

Porter, A., McMaken, J., Hwang, J., & Yang, R. (2011). Common core standards: The new U.S. intended curriculum. *Educational Researcher, 40*(3), 103–116.

Prensky, M. (2005). Listen to the natives. *Educational Leadership, 63*(4), 8–13.

Richard, K. (2011). Voices from the Ning: How social networking created a learning community in a young adult literature classroom. *The ALAN Review, 38*(3), 23–28.

Scharber, C. (2009). Online book clubs: Bridges between old and new literacies practices. *Journal of Adolescent & Adult Literacy, 52*(5), 433–437.

Skokie Public Library. (2012). *Multicultural experience: Books for teens*. Accessed at www.skokie.lib.il.us/s_teens/tn_books/tn_booklists/multcult.asp on February 22, 2012.

Stan, S. (Ed.). (2002). *The world through children's books*. Lanham, MD: Scarecrow Press.

Steiner, S. F. (2001). *Promoting a global community through multicultural children's literature.* Englewood, CO: Libraries Unlimited.

superkimbo. (2009, May 11). Technology in the MYP: The design cycle [online image]. Accessed at www.flickr.com/photos/superkimbo/3520372333 on February 20, 2012.

United States Board on Books for Young People. (2012). *Outstanding international book list.* Accessed at www.usbby.org/list_oibl.html on May 10, 2012.

U.S. Department of Education, Office of Educational Technology. (2010). *Transforming American education: Learning powered by technology.* Washington, DC: Author. Accessed at www.ed.gov/sites/default/files /netp2010.pdf on March 12, 2012.

Wagner, T. (2008). *The global achievement gap: Why even our best schools don't teach the new survival skills our children need—and what we can do about it.* New York: Basic Books.

Western and Northern Canadian Protocol. (2011). *Western and Northern Canadian Protocol (WNCP) for collaboration in (kindergarten to grade 12) education.* Accessed at www.wncp.ca/media/49521/protocol.pdf on May 9, 2012.

Yokohama International School. (2011a). *Achievement levels.* Accessed at www.yis .ac.jp/page.cfm?p=1833 on February 20, 2012.

Yokohama International School. (2011b). *IB diploma program.* Accessed at www .yis.ac.jp/page.cfm?p=763 on February 20, 2012.

Yokohama International School. (2011c). *Mission, values & aims.* Accessed at www.yis.ac.jp/page.cfm?p=9 on February 20, 2012.

Yokohama International School. (2011d). *The YIS Global Citizen Diploma Program.* Accessed at www.yis.ac.jp/page.cfm?p=1809 on February 20, 2012.

Zusak, M. (2007). *The book thief.* New York: Knopf.

INDEX

21st Century Skills
Edited by James Bellanca and Ron Brandt
Examine the Framework for 21st Century Learning from the Partnership for 21st Century Skills as a way to re-envision learning in a rapidly evolving global and technological world. Learn why these skills are necessary, which are most important, and how to best help schools include them.
BKF389

Bringing Innovation to School
Suzie Boss
Activate your students' creativity and problem-solving potential with breakthrough learning projects. Across all grades and content areas, student-driven, collaborative projects will teach students how to generate innovative ideas and then put them into action.
BKF546

Personal Learning Networks
Will Richardson and Rob Mancabelli
Follow this road map for using the web for learning. Learn how to build your own learning network. Use learning networks in the classroom and make the case for schoolwide learning networks to improve student outcomes.
BKF484

The Connected Educator
Sheryl Nussbaum-Beach and Lani Ritter Hall
Create a connected learning community through social media and rediscover the power of being a learner first. The authors show you how to take advantage of technology to collaborate with other educators and deepen the learning of your students.
BKF478

Solution Tree | Press
a division of
Solution Tree

Visit solution-tree.com or call 800.733.6786 to order.